Trustworthy Liars

A Fishing Memoir

Larry Meath

"...of all the liars among mankind, the fisherman is the most trustworthy"
William Sherwood Fox, *Silken Lines and Silver Hooks*, 1954

Contents

Map of the Area

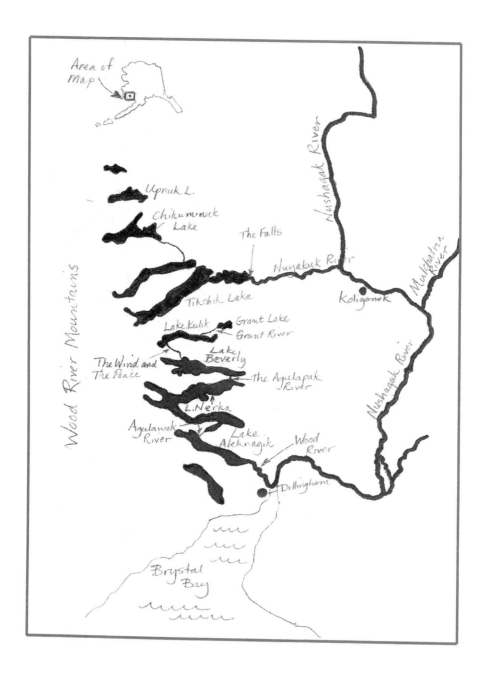

Preface

Fishing catches people in different ways. There is something primordial about throwing a hook and feathers into a river and tricking the denizens of the deep that it is in their best interests to chase and consume this artificial meal. But even after thrashing the water for hours and coming up empty handed, a reward still occurs in the process. Standing in a gin clear stream, watching the infinite patterns of water flow endlessly by, a hatch of mayflies glistening in the sunset, the rhythms of the cast ending with the line stretching across the river in a tight U as the fly gently floats down to the surface—these are magic moments. Fishing is all that—catching is merely a bonus; a reward that always elicits joy and amazement. Watching a grayling, rainbow, or any fish—for that matter—rise from the bottom of the stream and snatch a fly only to explode in surprise as the hook is set and the battle begins is a drama that never ceases to delight. It is even better, when in the end you release him back to the water to recoup and live for another day. And...still better if the fish is large—and your friends witness the whole thing.

The first time I saw the movie *A River Runs Through It* the fishing scenes immediately made me think of SW Alaska and my subsequent 25 or so years of fishing the streams and rivers with two great lifelong friends. Norman Maclean caught much of the spirit, the "Zen" of fishing, in his novelette. My storyline is not so tragic; the characters perhaps not so heroic; but the images of the joy of fly fishing in that movie caught the moments that remain frozen in mind from my own personal memories.

So, what follows is a series of adventures and life's lessons, mostly with two special friends with whom I had the good luck to share approximately 25 years of fishing trips to SW Alaska. Each summer, with rare exceptions, the three of us settled upon a date and planned and executed a trip where the main goal was simply to catch fish.

This is a fishing memoir. Others may write more knowledgably about habitat, technique, and the nuances of catching trophy fish, but they haven't shared the personal experiences and insights gained from 25 years of fishing with my two buddies. More importantly, no one can appreciate the massive amounts of shit that we piled on each other at every opportunity, thickening our skin and intensifying our resolve. As will become apparent, fishing with us was not for the weak of heart. No matter, if needed we would be there for one another without a secondary thought.

But in fairness, I need to start a bit earlier. Others have had huge influences directly and indirectly on my life and these stories. And so they need to be mentioned as well even though they may play a smaller role in the centerpiece of these narratives—our annual migrations to the Tikchik Lakes area of SW Alaska—the holy waters of fishing for many who have shared the experience.

This book is loosely organized chronologically around those trips to SW Alaska beginning in the mid 1980's. Each summer we repeated the process of organizing and equipping ourselves for anywhere from 8-12 days of non-stop fishing, weather permitting. And while many similarities existed from trip to trip, each one was unique in its own way. The goal, though, remained the same from year to year: catch big rainbow trout.

For the uninitiated, Alaskan rainbow trout exist primarily in the southern regions of the state south of the Alaska Range.

I have no background in biology, but what I've learned over the years is that the only rainbows north of the Alaska Range are mainly stocked fish in lakes and a few streams. While grayling inhabit all of the state, rainbows—our fish of choice—are more select in their habitat.

Wild rainbows typically follow the huge runs of salmon as they make their way up river systems to their spawning grounds. These trout greedily gobble eggs of the spawning salmon as well as other opportune feed in the water while they follow the salmon upriver. The rainbows that later return to the sea—steelhead trout—grow even larger, often reaching sizes over 30 inches in length. Local rainbows, those who stay in the lakes and streams closer to home, tend to be smaller.

Other prized sport fish share these waters and opportunistically feed on salmon eggs as well. Dolly Varden and Arctic Char are basically the same fish, the latter tending to range the coastal areas further north. It takes a skilled eye to tell them apart—they look virtually the same to me—and my partners and I use both names interchangeably. Species like pike and whitefish inhabit most of the state but we do not care much about fishing for them. Grayling are ubiquitous in Alaska, and even though they are not our fish of choice on these trips, they are always fun to catch for both their fighting ability and their unique beauty.

Alaska has a number of major river systems, but the largest, the Yukon, is rainbow trout free despite huge (albeit diminishing) numbers of salmon that make their way up its prodigious length. Again, the trout tend to stay in the southern part of the state, probably because propagation is difficult in the northern regions, and consequently the coastal areas of Alaska are dotted with hundreds if not thousands of lodges open seasonally for fishermen on once in a lifetime dream vacations. We were lucky enough to do this every year.

But really, this storyline is not so much about catching lots of big fish as it is about the logistics of those trips. The fish were merely the icing; the people made the experiences noteworthy.

1

My Fishing Roots

I've fished pretty much all my life. Having said that, I cannot claim to be one of those who lives, eats, and breathes to fish. This is perhaps the wrong way to start out a fishing memoir, but I have to be honest. When I'm on a river, especially on a glorious Alaskan summer day with the sun shining, the river rippling by with water so clear that even from a distance you can watch the fish rise off the bottom to snatch the fly, nothing could be better. However, when I compare myself to some of my fishing buddies, I just don't measure up.

My good friend Bob Olsen and I frequent the local fishing holes together regularly. "Local" is perhaps misleading because in reality our "hole" is 100 miles away, but we've made the trip so often it seems an easy journey. The river is appropriately named the Clearwater. This spring fed creek flows year round, never actually freezing except near the shoreline—even in harsh Alaskan winters where temps can easily be -50 Fahrenheit. Conversely, the river never warms much above freezing in the summer, staying consistently mind-numbing (and balls numbing) cold unless we are appropriately dressed. We do occasionally see other fishermen going by in boats, but for the most part we have the river to ourselves—which makes the experience all the better.

Bob is the kind of fisherman I'm not. We both love to fish, but he is a true student of the sport. Like most everything he does, he does it thoroughly and well. Bob ties better flies than I could hope for—let alone tie—my fly box is replete with his intricate creations. His casting makes me look like a novice—he can cast both farther and more accurately and has shown me many times how he can shoot every last inch of line, leaving only the backing on his reel while my feeble attempts end in a tangle of line by my feet. He buys only the best gear, and his reel bag is a treasure trove of top-end engineering marvels. In fact, Bob is, among other things, indirectly responsible for this book.

I was in Anchorage on business when I heard the news. Mutual friend Bill Bjork called me on my cell phone to let me know that Bob had been medivacced by jet to Anchorage with an aneurism. By the time I arrived at Providence Hospital where his wife and in-laws had gathered, he was in an induced coma with a tangle of wires and tubes emanating from his body. The neurosurgeon's prognosis indicated that the likelihood of a full recovery would be slim. He went on to say that Bob would probably sustain a serious disability—if he survived the operation: grim news.

Flash forward two weeks—after four hours of brain surgery and lengthy convalescence in ICU, Bob greeted my wife Stephanie and me warmly when we flew to Anchorage and returned to the hospital to see him. He still had a long way to go, but lying in bed surrounded by fishing magazines, I knew he was headed in the right direction. Our conversation immediately hit upon the topic of stalking trout, and he reminded me of new rules regarding wading boots and myxobolus cerebralis, the parasite commonly spread by fishermen on the felts of their boots. The fact that he could remember the Latin name impressed me: the fishing part of his brain still functioned perfectly. And while others functions took slightly longer to recover, Bob is once again playing bass (the standup musical instrument—not the fish) in the symphony, and more importantly, flogging the waters of lakes and rivers with his fly rods. Other than a dent in his baldpate where a silver dollar sized hole was cut and replaced, he is back to normal.

Two years later at a celebration of that recovery with Bob's visiting relatives from Wisconsin, Ed Thompson and I were talking fishing while tasting fine wines and delicacies in Bob's honor. Ed, a retired Proctor and Gamble VP was then dating Bob's older sister, and since I had a captive audience I regaled him with a couple of fishing stories. Ed is one who does not mince words, so upon hearing of my experiences he stopped me abruptly in mid sentence.

"Write a book."

"Naw, fishing books are dime a dozen...who would read it?" I replied.

"Write a book...you'd be surprised...this is the kind of thing people love to hear...." Ed went on convincingly, especially since my senses were a bit dulled and my ego boosted from the Martinelli pinot noir we were sharing. I dismissed the conversation as the festivities continued and smiling family photos took precedence.

The next morning I awoke somewhat hung over and after a medicinal dose of coffee, I opened my laptop to check my email. Before I knew it, I found myself suddenly pounding the keyboard and penning my fishing thoughts onto a Word program. Suddenly the pages started to fill up. The rest, as they say, is history.

But I need to finish my introduction to Bob. He subscribes to numerous fishing magazines like "Fly Rod and Reel," "Fly Fisherman," and "Salt Water Fly Fishing," and when we are together, which is often, the conversation usually involves an article or pictures from one of those publications. The pictures he calls "fish pornography"—they typically show a smiling face on a river, lake, or ocean setting, proudly displaying an obese fish of unbelievable dimensions—a hog in fishing parlance— usually held at arm's length, an old trick to make the fish appear even bigger. The pages are tabbed with orange sticky notes and the conversation is always the same— "We need to go there," he says. The places are usually exotic by fishing criteria: Christmas Island, the Kamchatka Peninsula, Belize, and even venues in in our own state. Bob has been to Christmas Island at least three times. I have yet to fish outside of Alaska.

Bob is way more astute about fishing than I, including some of the more practical nuances. For example, he involved his wife Dori in the sport early in their marriage, equipping her with the same top of the line gear so that when they are on the river, even if the catching is poor, they look impressive. I subscribe to the stereotype that many if not most women do not want to be caught dead in unfashionable gear. But the outfit is not purchased for that reason—Bob simply believes in quality, and his wife is the beneficiary of that philosophy. Furthermore, whenever I hear about their trips, he always gives Dori credit for the biggest or the most fish, whether true or not. Having a wife who is 100% behind your fishing trips simplifies things immensely.

So in comparison I'm a piker. The only reason I have gear of any quality is due to his coaching and expertise, or because I stumbled on a 20% off sale during a purchase. I tie flies, but the ones I use most are his. And the main reason we go fishing is because of his urging, "Let's sink a line—Wednesday is supposed to be beautiful and the grayling are in."

Unfortunately this fishing partnership occurred relatively late in my life. Even though we've been friends and acquaintances for over 30 years, our fishing exploits together did not materialize until after I had made several trips to SW Alaska fishing for rainbow trout. I could have greatly benefited from his advice the first time I traveled there.

I fish because I love it, but clearly, if not spurred by some outside influence, I might very well be too lazy or preoccupied with other trivial duties—mowing the lawn, working on a project, or watching golf on TV. A true fisherman would acknowledge that my values are skewed in the wrong direction.

My dad, a banker by profession, loved sports, especially, as local writer John Hewitt would call them, the blood sports—hunting and fishing. We had cabins devoted to those pastimes that our family owned, shared, or used in various places in Interior Alaska. We were not wealthy by any stretch, and the cabins were utilitarian and primitive, built from local spruce logs with no modern conveniences. Pumping up Coleman lanterns and splitting kindling were common chores for me at a young age, having first been cautioned about the dangers of both. I still bear a faded scar on my hand because of a close encounter with a sharp axe.

But these trips were the gist for father/son bonding. I was taught young how to fish, and since my dad (and namesake) was a fly fisherman, so was I. We only fished for grayling, and due to their abundance, I met with early success, but I truly can't remember much in the way of instruction from him. Perhaps this is due to the vagaries of memory, but it feels like I was self-taught even though logic would argue otherwise.

I do remember he taught me how to use a shotgun for duck hunting as a young boy, but unfortunately I was always paired with a spoiled brat about my age, the son of my dad's work associate and my partner in many of our hunting and fishing trips. His impatience at sitting in a duck blind for lengthy spells encouraged his dad to run us around in a boat ground-sluicing hapless birds too slow to get out of the way...a practice both illegal and unethical.

"Give 'em hell," my dad's friend would shout from the helm of the riverboat as he tried to run down the migrating creatures. My hunting partner had a disability: today he would have been diagnosed as dyslexic or possibly A.D.D. I'm guessing. This provided excuses for his excesses of behavior by those around him, especially his parents, but only frustrated me with my unsympathetic attitude toward juvenile justice. In time I became so discouraged by his antics (he especially liked to blow things up and kill squirrels for sport) that I lost interest in those trips and eventually found excuses to stay home. But when I hunted with my dad, the two of us would sit in a blind with decoys and quietly wait for the unmistakable sound of ducks feathering their wings in a landing. Those events were infrequent, though, and I never really learned how to shoot well.

But fishing was different. On a river I could separate myself from my hunting partner. Besides, fishing bored him so I found solace from the fact that he was uninterested and would spend most of the time lighting firecrackers elsewhere or pursuing some other more exciting activity, usually at an unsuspecting squirrel's expense.

I do remember that my dad showed me how to tie on my flies and leader, the basics of casting, and no doubt many other nuances of fly fishing, but few of these events remain seared in my mind. I can still picture him, though, wearing a fedora and sagging hip boots, his pipe in his mouth, and standing in knee-deep water casting into the riffle and drifting his fly—quietly enjoying the moment. He was a good father in most respects, but we were not particularly close, which bothers me when I think about it, and so fishing, as much as I enjoyed it was for a variety of reasons something that became less and less important to me as I grew older and became smarter than my parents, like all teenagers.

As the youngest of three, the baby of the family, my mother spoiled me, but my dad, never one to show much emotion, always seemed distant in comparison. My brother Bob was a generation older than I...a full 8 years...and my hero growing up. His athletic accomplishments dwarfed mine, and my coaches often called me by his name, a source of both pride and dismay. When my brother eventually tired of going hunting and fishing, my dad began to take me.

Kids on these trips were best to watch and listen, and follow orders. Alcohol was an integral part of the adult world, and I learned early on what happens in camp stays in camp. My dad later tolerated my own excesses...smoking pot in college...skipping classes extensively and flunking out as a freshman—so I can't complain of heavy-handed treatment. In fairness, I was probably the problem—not my parents— although that realization among others took years to sink in. Hindsight is amazing that way.

My dad's eventual blindness due to complications from diabetes bonded us to a certain extent. He did surprisingly well despite his disability, and his positive attitude was inspiring. Alcohol became a thing of his past, and his happiest moments seemed to be listening to the radio, especially baseball games where vision was not required. Unfortunately the disease also took a toll on his heart, and he died way too young at age 69. It was only years later that I began to fully realize how much I missed him and those moments we had together—especially fishing for grayling.

Fortunately, he was around for my wedding and he witnessed that I did eventually grow up and become responsible...mainly due to my wife's influence. After our marriage Stephanie and I returned to college where I completed my masters and received my teaching license, and soon we were back in Fairbanks, buying a home and working toward the American Dream. As usual, Stephanie was the motivator, and that included ideas about recreation. Fishing came back into my life as a result.

At her urging, we took up canoeing, and a necessary part of that enterprise included fishing—for food as much as fun. Success with a fly rod became a critical component of those trips. We bought a 15-foot Grumman shoe keel whitewater canoe and literally launched our summers into the water.

Most of our canoe trips were 2-3 days in length, sometimes longer, and eating fish was typically planned as part of our menu for half of our dinners. Our first forays took place on the upper Chena near our home, mild by whitewater standards but scary enough for inexperienced canoeists due to tight corners, sweepers (fallen trees hanging over the river's edge) and occasional rapids. Soon we graduated to the Gulkana River with sections of class III and brief stretches of class IV water.

Our first trip on the Gulkana nearly ended in disaster when after an exhausting couple of days with little sleep in our borrowed leaky tent, we tackled an 11-mile stretch of class III water. Our boat was the last one to take off, probably due to my anxiety and inexperience, and immediately Steph yelled, "Rock straight ahead!" The current quickly carried us toward it so I yelled from my position at the stern, "Right...go to the right." This took us on a more direct path to disaster and admittedly, in my somewhat inexperienced and panicked state of mind, I actually confused right with left. Stephanie turned around screaming, my navigational skills in question, and somehow we ended up perched backwards precariously high and dry on that huge bolder in the middle of the river with the swift current racing by us. Had a divorce attorney been available, I'm sure we would have signed the papers then and there. However, amidst all the yelling we managed to extricate ourselves without tipping over and somehow elatedly survived the remainder of the stretch.

In the end the trip exhilarated and excited us, and it was proclaimed a huge success, that is until we were driving back home and Stephanie realized she had left her wedding ring at our last campsite. We disagreed about the size of the diamond, which we never recovered—my estimate larger than hers.

The loss of the ring did not dissuade us from other canoe trips, though, and while we had many close calls, we never dumped, not even with our huge German Shepherd Max occasionally creating instability by excitedly standing up mid stream. Fresh caught grayling typically became the meal of choice every other day on the river, and fly fishing became a cherished part of those trips as we served fresh fish right out of the stream.

I was lucky to marry someone with a spirit of adventure. In our 40 plus years of marriage, most of the hiking and canoeing ideas came from her. And so as a result of all this, I gained a newfound love for fishing on those frequent canoe trips, usually with friend and neighbor, Jack Wilbur, as well as others we knew. For many years we planned at least one major canoe trip each summer along with several smaller events and day trips, and thus fishing became a standard part of the logistics for the planning and execution of these events.

2

The Green Goddess

So when Jack Wilbur first told me about his fly fishing trip to Southwest Alaska, pure envy filled my brain. Alaska is a big state and despite living here all my life, I had never actually experienced much of it first hand—including the entire SW region. The state road system is minimal by other states' standards, and travel to remote locations is expensive and often difficult—typically available only by small plane.

The rivers of SW Alaska are revered for fishing, and even though I knew little about the area—the fishing, the geography, or much else for that matter, I did know that this was where celebrities and VIPs went to catch lunker rainbows, huge char, and other species of fish common to the area—species I had never fished let alone caught. I don't remember the occasion of Jack's revelations, probably a dinner party at his house in 1985, but I do remember thinking how much I wanted a chance to throw my line into a river full of legendary fighting fish.

Other than an occasional foray drifting eggs for king salmon, my fishing experiences had been primarily limited to grayling in interior Alaska's streams and rivers. Not that grayling are disappointing, but the trout prevalent in SW Alaska were the stuff of legends. I really knew nothing about fishing for rainbow trout, char, or even fly fishing for salmon except for what I'd gathered from Saturday afternoon outdoor shows on television. My techniques and understanding of fly fishing were admittedly both antiquated and Philistine, having been raised using a Shakespeare automatic reel and the ubiquitous mosquito for nearly all my fishing. I had by this time upgraded to a decent Fenwick 5 weight fiberglass rod, but I continued to use my dad's old spring wound automatic reel.

Jack and two other lifelong friends, Bob Groseclose and Jamo Parrish, had made the initial trip at Jamo's invitation. Jamo (actually born James, but Jamo is the only name I had ever heard him called since we were in 8th grade together) and his brothers, partners in the family law firm, had purchased a new Cessna 185 on floats, a bush plane common in Alaska. Like many Alaskan outdoor lovers, they realized that the easiest and sometimes only access to great fishing and hunting was by airplane. And while charters are readily available, the convenience of having your own floatplane opened up the entire state for untold adventure. Also, they had convinced themselves after a couple of close calls at the hands of experienced charter pilots that they could manage just fine on their own. In one incident Jamo's brother Nelson watched in horror as a pilot aborted a poorly planned takeoff and planted the floatplane high and dry on terra firma on the opposite shore. Fortunately no one was hurt, but that pretty much sealed the deal to fly themselves around the state instead of relying on others of questionable skill.

Attorneys and doctors have a reputation, real or not, for being lousy pilots, mainly because it is a pastime and not an occupation, I suspect. Bad things can happen in a hurry in a small plane since hard landings tend to be unforgiving, and while it is probably unfair to single out those professions, the fact remains that Alaska is filled with amateur pilots and weekend warriors who head off to remote cabins without a thought to danger. So after the Parrishes purchased the plane that would cart them around the state, they partnered with another local attorney to acquire land on Suvarik Island in the Bristol Bay area of SW Alaska. Soon thereafter they commissioned a cabin to be built for their stays to the area.

Jamo was an experienced outdoorsman, canoe and kayak enthusiast, and as a result of a float trip years before down the Nushagak River he had familiarized himself with SW Alaska and the fishing possibilities. That first river float with his wife and others had spawned his initial interest and no doubt his determination—which eventually led to the purchase of the family floatplane, the cabin, and many years of great fishing as outlined in subsequent pages.

Jack, Jamo, Bob, and I all knew each other from school, family ties, church, etc., but more recently from canoe trips on a number of rivers in the interior of Alaska. Jack had actually been the impetus for the purchase of our first canoe that carried Stephanie and me on many successful voyages and tested our marriage on numerous occasions. When Stephanie told me of the whitewater trips our friends had been doing, the next step was to join ranks and buy a canoe.

Bob Groseclose was already somewhat of a legend to many of us. Bob embraces life with a wide grin on his face and a perpetually positive outlook—despite incredible family setbacks that would break most anyone. His mother, who had single handedly raised the family for many years working as a nurse, was tragically killed by a reckless driver in an automobile accident along with Bob's younger brother and sister while Bob was in college. Later, his older sister, Peggy, a classmate and friend of mine who went on to become a nurse herself, died in a private plane accident while still in her 20's. As devastating as all this was, Bob finished college, law school, and returned to Fairbanks to enter a law firm with his new wife, Barbara, also an attorney.

Bob is a Herculean hiker: he thinks nothing of embarking on wilderness "iron man" jaunts of 150 miles or so, racing cross-country over wild Alaskan mountain ranges and down raging rivers, surviving only on handfuls of granola. Big things come in small packages—his diminutive frame tips the scale at about 140 pounds soaking wet, but his ability to gut it out under grueling conditions puts him in a rare class. Hiking with him is not for the weak of heart, but canoeing with him is a pleasure since river current and not his pace dictates the speed of the journey. His boat of preference back then was a butt-ugly 17 foot Sawyer canoe dubbed the Phoenix for the unsightly patch-job Bob had applied to resurrect it after sinking it on an Interior whitewater river. Function took priority over "pretty" in Bob's worldview.

So when Jack told me about their fishing trip, I immediately pictured giant rainbows leaping in slow motion and tail walking across swift riffles; a plethora of fighting fish on each bend of the river—a preponderance of fish pornography photo ops. Growing up in Fairbanks in the 1950's we were spoiled as kids learning to fish. The rivers were so replete with grayling that we would often literally catch two fish on every cast. Tying a double mosquito setup on the line was about the only skill required. However, the gradual influx of human population to the area and greater access to rivers via the local road system had diminished that description somewhat even though rivers still secretly existed where the fishing was legendary. The "catch" was that finding the fish required a bit more work since anything accessible by road had a tendency to get fished out.

Other than salmon, grayling dominated as the fish of choice around Fairbanks and were, as previously stated, easy to catch on flies. However, spinning rods with small lures like a Mepps slayed grayling, literally and figuratively. And while most fishermen did not practice catch and release when I was growing up, fish caught on a fly like a mosquito or a gnat at least had a chance of survival if you chose to return them to the river. The treble hooks common to most lures were another story, and as a result fish mortality was typical when fishing with spinning rods—hence the demise of the stock over time. But back then fish mortality was never a concern: like everyone we knew, we kept our fish and ate them. That was the purpose of fishing. The only released fish were those considered too small, which ironically probably only sped the reduction of fish numbers since the big spawners were the ones kept and served for dinner.

However when I asked about it, Jack related to me that the fishing wasn't really all that great on that first trip to SW Alaska. They caught some nice fish, but my bubble was burst by the news that there were days where only a handful of fish were caught and landed, and even then only after much effort. In fact, even the grayling fishing was only average.

This did not register with the picture portrayed by numerous fishing shows I had seen on television where salmon-sized rainbows and char or dolly varden were featured in dizzying aerial displays, head-shaking and dancing across the water with fishermen whooping and hollering in excitement and rods bent double. Even edited footage could not hide the fact that legendary fishing occurred in these waters.

A 13-pound rainbow hung on the office wall of my father-in-law from a trip to Lake Illiamna in SW Alaska around that same time period. I could not look at this fish without awe, and every time I stepped in his office I would stare at that trophy posed in a mid-air fight to spit out the hook. The pictures of his trip showed a smiling party of bedraggled and grizzled fishermen holding a stringer of huge rainbows. Jack Wilbur's story of his first trip didn't compute. Either he was holding out—doubtful since I could pose no threat to any secret spots—or my ideas of the area resulted from a vast media conspiracy to deceptively lure unwitting fishermen to Alaska.

Even more unbelievable to me—Jack related that they didn't keep any fish. This was anathema—what was the point? Catch and release for most Alaskans at the time was a Greenie conspiracy. Jack's shoulder shrug led me to believe he had not totally accepted this new philosophy. Little did I know how soon I would change my take on releasing fish.

Of course I pressed for details regarding the trip: where they stayed, the flight there—the logistics of the adventure. The gist of Jack's response—"The cabin was great...the flight was long...the fishing was ok...but all in all, it was great." Despite his mundane reply I salivated inwardly like a dog staring at a steak.

3

The Genie Comes Out of the Bottle

The following year to my surprise I received a phone call from Jack, "Larry, are you interested in going to Dillingham?"

"What? Are you kidding me?" I was incredulous. "For real?" My mind began whirling at the thought.

"Bob can't go...so Jamo wanted to know if you were interested. We have an extra seat in the plane."

"Of course I'm interested. Give me the details."

Bob Groseclose was not really much of a fisherman: he preferred hiking to fishing, and in fact apparently did much of that while on the previous trip, choosing difficult hikes to mountain tops through thick brush rather than fish for giant rainbows, but regardless, he was unable to go and the plane had an empty seat. Overjoyed at my good fortune and shedding no tears over Bob's scheduling conflicts, I jumped at the opportunity. To this day I'm thankful that Bob prefers hiking 150 miles overland with only raisins and oat flakes, a map, and a positive attitude instead of standing in a crystal clear river catching fish. And after a brief and cursory discussion with my wife as a matter of marital diplomacy (in fairness, she did not hesitate in her agreement that I should go), I immediately began preparations for the trip.

Jack filled me in on the particulars, more detailed now than our previous discussion. We needed to buy all the food for 9 days—keeping weight to a minimum for the long flight—and assemble our personal supplies and fishing equipment since once at the cabin we would be unable to retrieve anything forgotten. I was like a kid nervously waiting for Christmas. I started making lists, and it soon became clear I would have to purchase a number of items missing from my gear bag.

The rivers and streams near Bristol Bay are heavily forested with brush and trees, or as is often the case, they run through low-lying swampy areas. Roads and even trails are non-existent in most places. Walking through the woods is typically difficult at best and often impossible except for short stretches due to thick brush and deadfall. Therefore, whenever possible we would be walking directly up many shallow river bottoms. I owned a pair of hip boots that I typically used for fishing, but Jack assured me that hip boots were worthless for the walking required down there since wading often required traversing waist deep water. So I ended up buying a pair of heavy, rubber chest waders.

Having never owned or worn a pair of waders before, I had no idea what I was getting myself into. Rubber waders are fine for standing more or less in one spot and the fact that they came to my armpits reassured me that I could navigate deep water, but Lord help me if I fell. I had enough room in them for two of me, and filled with water they would become a sea anchor. They were stiff, awkward, and hiking in them, as it turned out, countered any positive quality previously mentioned. I felt like I was wearing the proverbial barrel from a Laurel and Hardy movie. Naturally this revelation came too late since I only tried them on at home. Had I walked more that 20 feet in them, I probably would have thrown them away.

My Fenwick fiberglass 5 weight rod would do, but I needed a spare just in case. My wife's rod, a duplicate to mine, served that role, but my ancient automatic reel would be no match for a feisty rainbow, so I was encouraged to pack something heavier. I had previously built a 9-weight fiberglass salmon fly rod and purchased an appropriately sized Scientific Anglers reel and line. It was fine for the 9-weight rod, but affixed to my 5-weight Fenwick, it had the heft and look of a small winch.

"Do you have a motor for that reel? Jesus, we'll never get off the water with that thing in the plane. Better put a lead weight on your rod tip for balance...." Jamo mercilessly mocked my gear when he first saw it. The reel did give my rod the balance of an iron anvil on the butt end, and I believe my biceps grew in girth commensurate with the added heft.

My fly box had only grayling flies in it, typically #12 or #16 mosquitoes, a few fairy shrimp, (a fly Jack lives by) and a handful of commercially made novelty flies, but Jack assured me I would need bigger, heftier flies for the fish that we would be courting. As a result and after consulting various resources, I bought a half dozen or so muddler minnows that in the end proved to be of no worth, at least in my inexperienced hands. I eventually learned that the made-in-Taiwan versions I purchased were better as bobbers than wet flies. Instead of sinking and mimicking minnows, a delicacy for rainbows, they floated across the surface like small, swimming shrews. Years later we did have luck with other newer and better versions of minnow patterns, but I'm getting ahead of myself. My fly box, in short, was woefully inadequate, much like my knowledge of fishing for anything other than a grayling.

Jack and I were delegated to buy all the groceries, including adult beverages, for the trip. Loosely translated, this meant that I did all the shopping. As a teacher I had time off in the summer, and wanting to make a positive impression for the possibility of future trips, I agreed with the understanding that we'd square up later. Groceries were important, and Jack and I meticulously worked out a list of essentials—food items that would last the duration without being too heavy for the plane trip. Whiskey was at the top of the list—Jack drinks Canadian blends, typically R and R, while Jamo prefers American bourbon—Jack Daniels to be specific. I had not acquired a taste for whiskey, and beer was my beverage of choice, but beer is heavy and doesn't mix with airplanes and weight restrictions. So after purchasing at least nine days worth of supplies from our list and the assignations of Jamo, appropriately frozen and/or boxed for the trip, I picked up Jack in my Dodge truck and we headed for the airport.

Shortly after we arrived the bitching began. I was soon to learn this was a ritual that accompanied every trip.

Jamo was cordial but wore a worried frown as well. He had already completed the preliminary check of the plane, and his gear was piled on the ground awaiting our own before packing it all into the plane. He scrutinized the sky for weather, but mostly his concern focused on the glassy sheen of the float pond. The red and white Cessna sat quietly on its floats. Not a ripple occurred down the length of the water runway.

A Cessna 185 is one of the premier Alaska bush planes. It is a workhorse, and the Parrishes' plane was well equipped. It sat on a pair of huge white PK floats that, while not the most airworthy accouterments, provided considerable extra storage space. A STOL kit curved the wing tips downward, a feature relatively new to bush planes at the time, and one that aided flight. Nevertheless, Jamo tended to see the glass half empty.

"No fucking wind. An hour ago it was perfect and now, not a breeze." Other profanities accompanied this observation. Jack and I quietly awaited orders as we unpacked the truck and set the boxes of gear and supplies on the ground next to Jamo's pile. The rule of thumb was to keep things in small boxes for adjusting the load. Jack had most of his gear stowed neatly in a single, large, backpack.

"Christ, Jack. This thing weighs a fucking ton. What have you got in here?"

It had officially started. I kept my head down and continued to add to the pile by the plane from the gear in the back of the truck. Jamo had the hatch covers open on the roomy PK floats and was jamming anything small that could withstand possible dampness in them. We were admonished to walk only on the designated areas of the floats as he started loading the back of the plane and we ferried everything to him.

The plane's interior did not seem that big, but I was amazed at how much gear it could hold. Among other things we had a 15 horse outboard, paddles, miscellaneous items for the plane and all our gear and food for nine days or so. The rods were piled on top of the outboard engine and extended into the tail section where only light items could reside due to balance issues.

"How many fishing rods did you bring, Jack? I don't see how we'll ever get off the water...." It went on and on, but I kept my lips sealed. Finally, the plane reached capacity with gear still sitting on the ground. Jamo got on the phone and called Fred Barong.

Fred and Cheryl Barong were also flying down in their own plane, but since it was on wheels Fred could benefit from less friction, a longer runway, and hence, some of our weight. He already had our gas barbecue grill he was transporting, and after talking with Jamo on the phone, he ended up carrying some more of our gear as well. In time, we had everything loaded minus a few items Jamo could not see taking, which we left in the shed at the airport. The floats earned their name— but just barely.

We piled into the plane, me squeeeeezed in back and sitting on Jack's 100 pound pack (according to Jamo's exaggerated estimate) and Jack and Jamo in the front. I had a lap belt but no shoulder harness in the back seat...small comfort in case of anything going awry. I was assured that if we augured in the lap belt would work just as well as the shoulder harnesses. Jamo added to my solace, "Don't worry— it's only there to keep you from flying into us in the front seats. You'll probably die anyway." His reassurances provided little salve for my soul.

"Everyone ready...?" We nodded in the affirmative. Jamo opened the pilot's side window. "Clear!" he yelled as a matter of aviation protocol even though no one was outside the plane. He primed the engine, turned the key and the plane roared to life.

Airplanes are noisy—small airplanes more so. Soundproofing is essentially non-existent. I had a set of earplugs that moderately minimized ear damage, and Jack and Jamo wore headsets with mics for communication to each other but bypassing me altogether. Jamo goosed the throttle temporarily to slide the heavily weighted plane off the beach, and we slowly taxied out of our bay to the end of the float pond. Jamo checked in with traffic control and adjusted the altimeter as the big engine lugged along and warmed up.

"Fairbanks tower—Cessna six-one-four-seven-nine in the float pond ready for take off." Jamo communicated our departure with the tower, and once cleared, we taxied past the bright orange floats marking the end of the channel and turned around as close to the shore as possible, "The only good runway is the one in front of you," Jamo used this line repeatedly over the years. He rechecked the water rudders, yoke, and a few instruments, and then finally pushed the throttle to the firewall, nervously glancing skyward first.

The engine responded in kind, roaring loudly, and we raced...check that...slowly slogged down the pond. Acceleration occurred, but at an excruciating pace and seemingly in no relation to the thunderous noise from the engine. Ever so gradually the airspeed indicator started climbing toward the green mark that designated take off velocity, Jamo pushing and pulling on the yoke as we struggled to get the floats on step and skimming over rather than plowing through the water. I was leaning forward in the back seat in a vain effort to will us airborne. Using as much of the pond as we dare, the air speed needle finally hit the green mark and Jamo pulled back on the yoke. We popped off the water at last, flying tail heavy like a lead paperweight.

All of Jamo's complaining was rooted in good sense. Logic dictates that planes fly better light than heavy. And if we somehow had to abort the takeoff and survived the landing despite my inadequate lap belt, it might at least result in a ramp check from the FAA that could be problematic. So on this and virtually every other trip over the years we were reminded by the pilot that the plane was at or near gross weight with only a full tank of gas and our svelte bodies. Anything beyond that was extraneous as far as the manufacturer's recommendations were concerned, but we continued to defy the laws of gravity for that flight and others. Regardless, legal issues did exist concerning our weight and the pilot's culpability—and our lawyer/pilot never let us forget that.

Which brings me to the legal documents I had to sign before I could get in the plane—starting with a waiver absolving the pilot of any responsibility in the unfortunate event of my demise. Also, because I didn't have a will made out, I hastily had to write one on a napkin that I saved in some unknown location (years later Meg, the retiring secretary at the school where I worked retrieved the "napkin" last will and testament from the school safe and asked me what the hell THAT was all about). I most likely wrote more than one napkin will over the years, which could have created truly interesting issues for my heirs. Because the Parrishes were attorneys, anyone who flew in their plane had to sign a waiver releasing them of all liability. I read the first four words and ignored the remaining sixteen pages—much like a modern software agreement—not really knowing if I would be relinquishing my house and wife in the process. I desperately wanted to go fishing.

So, paperwork signed, plane in the air, we began the journey.

The first leg of the flight follows the Tanana River, a big muddy glacial-fed waterway with numerous channels and islands but providing a safety net of sorts in case a floatplane needs an emergency landing. It took seemingly forever to gain altitude, and even though we were comfortably airborne we stayed well below 1000 feet as we followed the river. Then something that became a regular feature of future flights happened—Jack fell asleep moments after we left the pond.

Jack, later the CEO of his engineering firm but back then simply a responsible employee, would typically pull all-nighters before the trip to get his work finished. This was a tact that I had abandoned after college, which by the way was essentially how everyone I knew survived term papers, final exams, and other requirements of university life. Life had allowed me to assume regular patterns of sleep, but not so for Jack. He typically arrived at work at 6 a.m. and would often put in marathon hours. This always came to a head right before our departure, so it was natural that he was exhausted at the onset. Add to this that he has a history of falling asleep anywhere at any time and it is no surprise he typically passed out within minutes of our departure.

The problem is that in the front seat he is the co-pilot in emergencies and, more importantly, serves as the lookout for other plane traffic. At one time Jack actually had a pilot's license paid for by Uncle Sam as part of the GI bill, and even though he never really flew after that, it made sense that he sit up front...but not if he couldn't stay awake for more than five minutes. Any reassurances we had of Jack's ability to land the plane in an emergency were countered by his loud snoring. So at Jamo's insistence Jack and I learned to switch places—in flight.

This might be best described as a game of Twister inside a garbage bag. Imagine two full-grown adults swapping front to back seats inside a Volkswagen Bug while traveling down the freeway and you'll get the idea. How we managed I'll never know, but in fact we did switch places and Jack was soon fast asleep in the back of the plane while I sat up front.

Jack is a distinct character. For all of his adult life he has sported a thick full beard to match his curly hair, once black but now grey. In this day and age he might be confused for an Arab terrorist despite his British Isles' roots as the beard gives him a slightly sinister countenance even though he is quick to smile. His glasses, however, moderate this somewhat by giving him a more intellectual look. Jack's stocky build equipped him well for rugged outdoor adventures like bushwhacking on overland hikes. He is a true Alaskan, never complaining about weather or much else for that matter—and always happy to be outdoors. Overall, Jack's demeanor is thoughtful and quiet most of the time...but especially so when sleeping soundly as he was now in his back seat nest.

My switch to the co-pilot's seat, I deemed, was a position of importance and I took my responsibilities seriously, scanning the horizon for Russian Migs, Boeing 747's, or whatever danger might come our way. Truthfully though, the real bonus to my new seat was that only the front seats had headsets and mics, and the person in back couldn't hear a thing other than any engine noise that bypassed the ear protectors...great for sleeping off an all-nighter, but lousy for three way discussions.

But back to that very first flight—Fred and Cheryl Barong had taken off just after us from the runway parallel to the float pond.

Fred contacted us over the radio about 10 minutes after take off, "Jamo, this is Fred—how are you doing?"

"We're just over the Tanana at 800 feet. How is it going with you?"

"We're still in ground effect but hope to gain a few feet so we can clear the river bank." It was the first of many shared lies based in fact and fear. We were both flying heavy, and taken literally, Fred's comment indicated he was no more than a few feet off the ground. We soon spotted him flying normally, but the radio chatter between the two planes continued to be filled with jokes and falsehoods—a non-stop 400 mile fable about all the game we were spotting: bear, sheep, caribou, moose, etc., none of which was true but allowed us to one-up each other and provide entertainment for the long flight.

If memory serves that first trip for me was long but relatively uneventful. After nearly 5 hours of wilderness flying we arrived at the cabin late that afternoon, unloaded the plane, and then Jamo flew over to the landing a few miles across the lake to pick up Fred and Cheryl. Since they were on wheels, they had to land on the strip at the village of Aleknagik and leave their plane there. For the remainder of the trip all of us were ferried around in Jamo's Cessna 185 to various fishing holes.

Another person was yet to join us: General Jim...a retired army veteran and helicopter pilot from the Viet Nam era who had provided expert testimony for the Parrish law firm in a liability suit dealing with helicopters. He was also a friend of the Parrishes and an avid fisherman. The General was the final complement to our crew—the cabin was full. We were ready to go fishing.

4

The Cabin

Cabin is a bit of a misnomer, especially as Alaskan "cabins" go. The word cabin in Alaska usually conjures an image of a one-room log structure with a wood stove that doubles for cooking, possibly along with a 2 burner Coleman stove. If it is truly authentic, it will have a sod roof and spruce burl support posts all of which are slowly sinking back into the tundra.

This cabin is really a two-story Lindal cedar structure, albeit with fundamental accouterments placed in a remote area. The cabin sits on a small island in the middle of Lake Aleknagik, the lowest of the Tikchik Lakes located about 15 miles from the town of Dillingham and Bristol Bay. The small Yupik village of Aleknagik sits

27

about two miles to the east of the island, but other than the school and Moody's Marina where we purchase avgas from Rollo Moody, a white haired octogenarian still humping heavy hoses to planes for refueling, the village is mostly comprised of somewhat ramshackle houses owned primarily by indigenous subsistence and commercial fishing families. Most of the houses are sided with painted plywood, weathered and peeling from the harsh elements. Lund skiffs dot the shoreline and 4-wheelers race up and down the trails that serve as streets. No one wears a helmet.

Just past the village, the lake narrows appreciably at its eastern extremity to form the Wood River, which flows into the Nushagak River at Dillingham in a broad delta. A road connects Dillingham with Aleknagik, but ends naturally at the lake where the landing serves many purposes—from the float plane pick-up and drop-off point for clients of the many fishing lodges in the area—to the town's boat launch for access to the lakes. The abundant fishing lodges that are scattered around the lakes and rivers are luxurious places with scenic views, rock fireplaces, and all the amenities of major hotels. They stand in stark contrast to the village houses. We never go in the lodges, and we would probably be unwelcome if we did. Their customers come from far and wide and pay a premium for the privilege.

The area in general is unsurpassed for stunning vistas, especially but not exclusively from the vantage of an airplane. To the west of the lakes lies the Wood River Range, a jagged saw tooth set of mountains separating the Tikchik lakes from the numerous rivers and small lakes of the Togiak River drainage. Sunsets are always inspiring, and flying to Lake Aleknagik on a summer evening never grows old as the waning sunlight glistens golden off the reflection from the lake.

The lake itself is dotted with numerous small islands, the habitat of houses and cabins of fishermen like ourselves along with year-round residents who mostly rely on commercial fishing for their livelihood. In the winter accessibility is much easier in some respects as the water becomes a vast snowfield and snow machines supplant boats as the transportation du jour.

Our home for these fishing trips is two stories: one large room on the ground floor used as kitchen, dining room, living area, and workstation for rigging gear. The upstairs loft, served by a steel spiral staircase in the center of the cabin, is simply a plywood floor, barren except for mattresses stacked against the walls.

"Grab a mattress and choose your spot," Jack instructed me. Each of us flopped a mattress on the floor, claiming our sleeping spaces, and rolled out our sleeping bags. The arrangement was simple and comfortable, and stayed basically the same for 25 or so years right down to the order of our beds. Pillows were stashed in garbage barrels for safekeeping and to keep dust off—the place was utilitarian and clean but not sanitized—as a cabin should be.

The downstairs also had a two-piece sectional couch, eventually occupied by Jamo for his bed—"It's too fucking hot upstairs." Doors were virtually never closed after we arrived—just the screens. Every time Jamo went out or in, he left the door wide open, which resulted in me closing it. Eventually tiring of watching me repeat this ritual, he admonished me, "Leave it open. It gets too hot in here to sleep." His internal furnace operated differently than mine.

"Just put on another layer," Jack advised. No matter the weather, the door would remain open.

Fires in the rusted wood stove were therefore non-existent—even looking at the wood stove started Jamo whining. "No fucking fires," we were informed. It was far better to freeze than to listen to him complain—a lesson repeated and respected over the years. Since the cabin doors remained open, warped homemade screen doors served as a barrier for sometimes-abundant mosquitoes and flies, and even bats that occasionally clung to the screens in the evening. Evidence of bugs from over the years existed in the form of numerous fly corpses, somehow trapped between the double panes of a large window, the glass cracked most likely from a too hot fire at one time in the stove perched in front of it. In general though, the bugs were not bad on the island and the gaps in the screen doors did not cause a problem.

The upper floor also had a narrow walkway leading from the sleeping loft to a flimsy second story deck where a 30 gallon or so water tank sat in the corner. We filled this tank with lake water that from a distance looked potable if you didn't pay attention to the dead fish, duck droppings, and miscellaneous flotsam and jetsam floating in the lake. Once the tank was pumped full, gravity then provided us with all our running water needs for cleaning and drinking. Various clever permutations to improve that system took place over the years, but from the start it seemed simple and effective and no one perished from the marginal sanitation standards.

The upstairs deck was also a convenient place for midnight peeing although the height of the 2x6 railing originally required an "over or under" decision based on the height of the person urinating. Since negotiating the narrow spiral staircase seemed precarious for sleepwalkers when duty called in the middle of the night, one had only to walk out onto the deck and pee over the edge, avoiding the railing for obvious sanitary reasons. Eventually a convenient block of wood became a rickety step to elevate the appropriate equipment at the proper height so we could pee over the railing without making a mess. This system was simple and functional as long as you were semi-awake during elimination of body fluids. A lengthy fall over the railing would probably go unheeded anyway and not waken the snoring bodies inside the cabin.

Rows of wooden pegs for hanging gear dotted the walls around each level of the cabin. The main floor also had the aforementioned unused wood stove, the sectional couch and accompanying chairs, and a kitchen with a counter and seating for approximately four, depending on the stool arrangement. A full sized Kenmore stove with a large oven cooked the meals, and a small propane refrigerator kept things cold and provided ice, a requisite for the whiskey. Finally, a large map of the area covered much of the north wall of the main floor and served as a research document for planning our fishing excursions.

In short, we had virtually all the comforts of home.

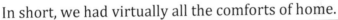

5

Electrical Tape—The Ultimate Fix

Since the cabin sat empty for much of the year and the only way to get supplies there was in the plane, nothing was thrown away except for perishable food items, a fairly common practice in "bush" Alaska where a critical nail or a bolt can be hard to find. Leftover food items were stored in large barrels inside the cabin and remained stuffed with flour, sugar, and sundry packaged goods.

Creating novel uses out of ordinary items was an everyday event. Repairs and updates were carried out each trip, and some huge tasks were accomplished with simple manpower and lots of ingenuity. The term jury-rigged has special significance, and with all due respect Jamo as an attorney was especially adept at the practice—he could creatively fabricate a solution for nearly any problem. A weed whacker was created from a joist hanger, a piece of wood, and electrical tape. It effectively cleared pathways for years until a gas burning replacement came along. Ear protection for me in the back of the plane was made from another extra joist hanger and blue foam attached with again—electrical tape. Over the years, I was continually amazed at the useful but always butt-ugly solutions he devised.

Duct tape is ubiquitous in Alaska. It is famous as fabric for wings when bears have attacked planes; it is glue for innumerable fixes: it takes care of leaks and it patches clothing...the list goes on and on. Jamo, on the other hand, showed utmost disdain for duct tape, preferring electrical tape instead, which after a fashion became his calling card. Electrical tape went everywhere with us. It was the proverbial Vegematic of quick fixes. As a result, it served as an inadvertent nametag for much of Jamo's equipment.

"All we need is a little electrical tape, and we're good to go." The faucet, the sink drains, fly rods, fly boxes...all were patched with electrical tape. When leaks developed we exchanged old tape with new applications. That and "ackumpucky," spelling unknown—which was the generic word Jamo used for shoo goo or other similarly adhesive gels or glues—the stickier the better.

Whenever we would come across something broken, mangled, or otherwise out of use, Jamo would quietly examine it, the wheels and gears turning, and disappear to the garage surfacing minutes later with an assortment of crude tools, screws, and the obligatory tape. Jack ignored all this movement unless called upon for help. As an engineer he could hold his own in the fix it department, but his input was usually more cerebral than physical. If absolutely required, he would get his butt off the couch where he would usually be sleeping with a book on his chest, and reluctantly proffer his advice. I usually joined in when it became too painful to watch.

Without trying to be boastful my "finish" skills were a notch or two above Jamo's. His creative solutions usually worked, but he operated by the bigger hammer approach much of the time. I would usually step in only after Jamo's engineering had me convinced that more layers of tape were not the solution and his efforts laid a guilt trip on me. Besides, both Jamo and I have a certain amount of nervous energy when it comes to projects, balanced by Jack who could successfully hold down any couch. Regardless, when something needed to be accomplished, we all three pitched in, but only if weather prevented us from getting out of the cabin to fish. Fishing was the priority except for emergency fixes.

Jack contemplating a solution

6

The Art of Trout Stalking

Jamo Parrish photo

Fishing was the reason we were there. And that first trip Jamo catered to each of us (our group had grown to 6 for that trip) by dropping everyone off at different places to fish. He loved to fly and these trips were his excuse to do so, but he also loved to fish and to be honest, he was typically the most successful fisherman in the group—although I would never admit that at the time. He spent much of that first trip dropping us off and then later picking us up at pre-appointed rendezvous.

Whenever we leave the cabin on Lake Aleknagik we typically fly north and head over the "saddle," a 500-foot high dip in the mountains separating Lake Aleknagik from Lake Nerka. As we gain altitude, the other islands come into view down the length of the lake, framed at the end by the Wood River Mountains towering in the distance. Lakes Beverly, Nerka, and Aleknagik are partially surrounded by smaller mountains, rounded and treeless on top but imposing nonetheless. The lakes themselves are formidable bodies of water, ten miles long or so east to west and relatively narrow in their north-south attitude. Their eastern perimeters typically extend into tundra and spruce, pocketed by hundreds of glacial pothole lakes, most no more than 10 acres in size. From the air the terrain deceptively resembles a lush emerald golf course. Uncounted rivers and streams crisscross the land in serpentine pathways, many of which are not navigable due to their small size. Walking across the land was another matter, however.

The perspective of the earth from the airplane at most any altitude is deceiving as great distances seem of little consequence. Add a glorious sunset (we rarely were up early enough to see a sunrise although we flirted with it from the other end a few times) and the experience is almost religious. In over 20 years we experienced this countless times. It wasn't something commented upon each time, but—guaranteed—the vastness of the land never failed to move each of us as we passed over it.

As previously mentioned Jack's sleeping in the plane (and elsewhere) was the stuff of legends. The airplane was his Valium. And while he invariably gave me his front row seat for the long trip down and back to Fairbanks because I did not suffer from narcolepsy, it was a point of personal pride for him to be in the jump seat while we were doing excursions from the cabin. Each time Jamo would chastise Jack about being vigilant and remind him that our lives were at stake: as remote at the area was there were plenty of planes flying around and they all tended to fly the same pathways around and over the lakes.

Jack swore allegiance, vigilance, alertness: you name it. We would load the plane with all our gear, pump the floats, prep the plane, and push off, but within minutes Jack would be out like a cheap prizefighter.

My perch in the back was typically a variety of makeshift seats: sometimes the inflatable raft, sometimes a fly box or a bucket...and over the years we learned to make it comfortable. In truth I loved sitting in back despite my isolation from any conversations. I probably read 40 novels over the years in my back seat nest, and I got my share of naps in too, clandestinely since front row eyes tended to be glued forward. Because I had no headset and no one could hear me back there, my vantage as a lookout was not a consideration. I would have to scream to make a point over the roar of the plane, so I tended to keep opinions to myself and resign my fate to those in front.

The severe criticism Jack suffered for his lackluster performance as a lookout bothered him I'm sure, but just not enough to keep him awake. To be honest he is a guy of considerable willpower and mental acuity and one of the smartest people I know. Nonetheless he could not resist the temptation to pass out in the plane and fix himself in what I would call the "guide" position.

The "guide" position involved leaning to the right and forward, head down in an attitude of one scrutinizing the earth as if looking for game. From the back seat, his position usually looked convincing; from the pilot's perspective—ditto. His head was usually turned just enough so his eyes were concealed by his feigned interest in the ground. But closer inspection always revealed the discrepancy: spotting anything is difficult with closed eyes. Bears, moose, caribou...all animals we regularly spotted from the plane...are INVISIBLE—with eyelids in the down position. I know this to be true because I have to confess that I employed the same techniques on a few occasions myself. Falling asleep in a noisily droning airplane is easier than you would suspect despite the admonishment from the pilot about the importance of being vigilant.

Jack in the guide position

However on this first day of fishing none of this took place. Jack was alert and attentive. Our first drop-off at a fishing hole turned out to be non eventful and certainly not life threatening, especially as far as the fish were concerned. Regardless, I could barely contain my excitement as I prepared to devastate the fish population with my fly rod.

Jack and I were paired up and dropped off at the mouth of a fairly small, slow moving stream that carved its way methodically through the tundra into Lake Nerka—about a ten-minute flight from the cabin. Jack wore a black rubber wet suit back then—the kind designed for snorkeling or cold weather diving but appropriated by him as practical for fishing. The wet suit lived up to its name: he not only got wet, he planned on getting wet, but the neoprene kept him warm in the process. While this is not typical fly-fishing gear, Jack considered it practical and efficient.

We jumped out of the plane, unloaded our rods and daypacks with lunch inside, and proceeded to cast into the slow moving water as Jamo flew off for the next shuttle. I was wearing my brand new previously described rubber chest waders, which weighed about 20 pounds but felt like 100. Immediately I discovered they were impossible to walk in, so when the fishing proved lousy at the mouth of the stream we started hiking up the riverbank where a small animal trail ran along the stream. At the beginning of the trip Jamo had loaned Jack a large chrome .44 handgun for protection, but I was unarmed. This fact hadn't bothered me until after marching for a few minutes, I realized too late there was no way I could keep up with Jack in his wet suit and hiking boots. Soon, he disappeared up the trail ahead of me, my noisy footsteps the only sounds I heard as I stumbled after him. I felt like I was walking with a plastic bubble around me when suddenly I came across a large hole in the bank, which I was sure had to be a bear's den.

Grizzly bears within 50 miles of the coast are generally regarded as Brown Bears in Alaska. They are the same beast—just bigger, scarier versions due to their diet of abundant salmon. The stuffed versions of these animals greet tourists and residents alike as they arrive at airports in Anchorage or Fairbanks, and their size is impressive. A can of bear spray feels highly inadequate when one thinks about a snarling bruin charging out of the brush at a speed roughly the same as a quarter horse. Those carnivorous beasts in our area had undoubtedly long-since vacated their dens and were roaming freely about, but the sight of the hole freaked me out and served as a reminder that we were clearly in bear country. My perceptions were also heightened by the absence of Jack's .44-

caliber revolver now several river bends ahead of me. My pace quickened despite the rubber body armor I was wearing. Finding Jack and not fish suddenly became my mission.

Admittedly I was a little panicked, but reason eventually took over even as I began sweating bullets from the effort to walk over swampy terrain while restrained by an oversized pair of rubber waders. Panic soon succumbed to exhaustion. Eventually I came around a corner and there stood Jack, calmly casting away in a stream that now had no current; it was as dead as the proverbial doornail—and even had a telltale layer of scum floating on the surface. Clearly he had no sense of the danger from which I had just escaped, and I didn't feel any compulsion to inform him—the proximity of the pistol had somewhat assuaged my fears and I saw no reason to advertise my anxiety. Our stream, now essentially a swamp, had yielded not a nibble and we both agreed there was little chance for fish to be lying around to make our day. After some token casting and unsuccessful attempts to get my floating muddler to sink, we finally agreed to head back in case the plane came by.

Eventually we were picked up and made it back to the cabin after some cursory scouting elsewhere with modest results. No one had had particularly good luck, but we later taxied across the lake to a small stream filled with spawning salmon and caught some nice dolly varden at the mouth of the creek. In fact the fishing was excellent by just about any standard, and it provided a welcome relief from the less profitable events of the day. The six of us finished the day on a high note, especially me. This was my first day fishing Bristol Bay waters, and while the mental film footage may not have won accolades from sport fishing enthusiasts, the fishing had progressed in the right direction.

Two of our group, Fred and Cheryl, ended up staying only a few more days, and too soon they said their good byes and flew back to Fairbanks, leaving Jamo, Jack, and me along with General Jim, who stayed a few days longer, to figure out where the big ones were lying.

7

Fishing the Agulapak

At one time the Agulapak River was chosen by famed sports' announcer Curt Gowdy as one of the all time great trout fishing streams in America, or so Jamo repeatedly claimed. Like many rivers in the Tikchik Lakes wilderness area, its short length belies a swift and sometimes treacherous current. The river connects two large lakes—Lake Beverly and Lake Nerka. In the approximately two miles of river between the lakes there are great pockets of water and sections of rapids that make for interesting wading and at times great fishing. Since it is a short flight to the river, it is a convenient place to go when the weather is not fully cooperating. The drawback is that it collects lots of guided fishermen, especially on days when the flying is marginal.

The river bottom is lined with smooth, grapefruit sized or larger boulders covered with green, slimy algae that requires sure-footedness and a bit of a death wish to get to the good spots. Add to this a noisy, swift current, probably about 5 miles per hour during normal water levels, and it can be a recipe for fun and/or disaster.

The lodge guides would typically motor into the mouth of the river at the outflow of Lake Beverly and either anchor or hold the boat in place while the clients fished from the platform of the flat-bottomed open vessels. Even though it is a big river, possibly a quarter mile across at the outflow of

Beverly, it can be fairly shallow, allowing one to carefully get a long ways from shore and still be in knee to thigh deep water. Rainbows and dollies follow the salmon going through the lake system, and at times the fishing has been outstanding. The downside is the presence of the aforementioned other fishermen, something we tried to avoid.

An old empty, uninsulated frame cabin sits on the eastern bank overlooking the river. In the summer, volunteers for the state park system live there and survey the fishermen. These typically young college students, outdoor recreation or biology majors usually, are living the dream in a beautiful wilderness setting.

Invariably they stop us and ask a few questions about our experience. The Tikchik lakes are part of a huge state park, approximately 1.6 million acres, and one of the first questions we are usually asked is, "How many people does it take to diminish the quality of your experience?" to which Jamo would always retort somewhat good-naturedly, "Do you mean other than you?" This is really a smart-ass answer, but in truth it is indicative of how spoiled we are in this wilderness setting. The fact that we have to share the river with guides and their clients is not something we cherish, and in fact we only did it when weather precluded us reaching other venues. That said, humility only goes so far, and if the fishing is fantastic we learned to sometimes swallow our pride and turn a blind eye to other fishermen. And occasionally we shared rivers where the fishing was spectacular—sometimes for everyone except us—a point not worth discussing.

Admittedly, over the years I have often been blinded by ignorance and inexperience when it comes to fishing. Our learning curve has often been slow and mine perhaps slower than others. Thus if a guided client is standing in a boat catching fish hand over fist and I am not, it is obviously because he or she is in a better spot or has "the" fly. The truth is that my technique was just ok, and patience not always my strong suit—if the catching is bad it is clearly a bad hole—or so I reasoned. Rainbow fishing, I soon learned, was not like that. We had to work for our fish, and even when the fishing was good it most often did not result in a hookup on every cast—not even in one of Curt Gowdy's top ten streams in America.

So when the college students surveyed us, we would invariably have a nice friendly chat with them before or after dipping our lines—after all, they were just doing their job, and they have that youthful charisma and energy. Plus, the girls were usually cute and presented a nice contrast to looking at each others' grizzled and unshaved faces.

On the other hand we rarely talk to the guides and never converse with their clients. This is not out of snobbishness from either them or us. They are paying way too much money to exchange small talk other than a wave of the hand greeting with the likes of us, and more importantly we seldom get close enough to be heard even if we wanted to talk to them. On the rare occasions when we did have an opportunity to talk to the guides, they were friendly. The short of it is though, we avoid going to streams where we have to share space just because we don't have to. It is a big country.

The Agulapak has yielded some great days of fishing nonetheless. And fishing there was worth it just to watch Jack inevitably fall into the river trying to get to that perfect spot. Wearing a wet suit while fly fishing implied that he was unafraid of getting wet. No doubt he was the cocktail hour talk at the lodge from clients who had recently exchanged their Orvis or Patagonia fishing gear for Dockers and tasseled shoes, "Did you see the guy in the wetsuit? What was THAT all about?" Little did they know Jack could get to almost anyplace accessible by the guides' riverboats...he was truly hard core when it came to catching fish, fashion be damned.

That first year though, he and I floated the Agulapak as did Jamo's friend, General Jim, during his short stay—Jack and I together in a four-man raft and the General in an inflatable kayak. Jamo unselfishly dropped us off and picked us up at the other end. As it turned out all the good fishing for rainbows was usually up near Beverly where the guides were, but we had great grayling fishing and occasional rainbow explosions further down the river. The outflow of the river at Lake Nerka consistently provided great dolly fishing when the current carried the salmon smolt into the lake. This provided a feeding frenzy for the opportunistic eaters, and even with my marginal skills early on, at times the fishing was a fury of whoops and hollers of delight. Invariably sea gulls shared our screams and bounty by diving into the water along side us and feasting on the minnows.

That first year in particular, I learned many lessons— lessons about fishing, lessons about gear, about flying, and lessons about myself. For the next 25 or so years Jack, Jamo, and I traveled back and forth to Aleknagik together. At times others joined us as with that first trip, but usually it was just the three of us. Occasionally there would be a hitch in the arrangement: I missed a few years over the decades and Jack only once, but basically it was an event I can safely say that each of us looked forward to every single year and thought about all year long.

Rituals are insidious. We do things over and over and suddenly they are part of us—for better or worse. We grew wiser (for the most part) as we grew older, and we certainly learned the hard way about fishing these waters. We were always experimenting with technique, flies, fishing holes, and gear. And of course we heaped shit on each other for good reason—or not—as guys are wont to do.

Along the way and over the years we shared great adventures. Every day was a new experience and we never tired of any of it. Even mundane cabin chores and routines had their thrilling moments or stood out for some reason—usually at someone's expense. Certainly much of this does not translate in meaningful ways to anyone other than the three of us. But then, often the things that strike us as insignificant resonate with others.

At any rate, a few of our experiences follow.

8

Creating Routines

The cabin on the island in Lake Aleknagik provided a safe haven as well as most of the creature comforts for us. We were blessed with running water—of sorts, a great stove, refrigeration, cooking utensils—all the basics. If we needed something we found a way to make it. That first year I carved a large, crude "spork" for cooking since we were without any wooden cooking utensils. This ugly but useful implement is still in service to this day. Jamo's wide ranging skills included concocting just about anything edible from simple ingredients, a requirement when we forgot key food items, but despite his considerable cooking talents, Jack and I generally handled the culinary chores. Jamo was the "griller" —he owned the grill, but most everything else in the kitchen was split between Jack and me.

Our menus were virtually the same every year. Lack of complaints invited repetition. Like many men, our meals were unimaginative and basic (some might even say boring), but simple and enjoyed immensely. More importantly though, we cooked everything more or less from scratch...no premade, canned, or instant meals like MRE's. Jack's traditional dinner delights included pea soup, beans and ham hocks. Among my creations were pasta with clam sauce, stir fry Chinese, and breakfasts.

Sourdough pancakes topped with homemade blueberry syrup started us every other morning. Store bought blueberries elicited howls of complaint: they had to be wild Alaskan berries famous for their tart flavor. Days without Sourdough pancakes began with bacon and eggs and flipping the eggs without the use of a spatula became a requirement first started by Jamo. Both Jack and I failed at this initially, and Jack's attempts were hit and miss for many breakfasts over the years resulting in mangled eggs and accompanying epithets.

The art of sourdough pancakes

The secret lay in the arm motion—and lots of olive oil. A jerky toss or a failure to commit to the process resulted in broken yolks along with humiliation and jeering. Jack simply tried too hard, and his attempts to save the toss invariably brought Jamo into the kitchen to "school" him in egg flipping.

While guacamole may seem ordinary as an appetizer, ours was not—early on we became addicted to guacamole infused with hot peppers. Every night upon returning to the cabin the order of events was the same...unload and tie down the plane. Carry all the gear inside, get the booze from the secret storage spot, get out the ice, and watch Jack prepare the guacamole.

First he drizzled olive oil into the fry pan; then he added about a dozen red chili peppers. The oil would be heated until the chilies were literally smoking and the room was rendered unbreatheable from the choking fumes. While the chilies were cooking, several avocadoes would be mashed together with mayonnaise. Finally, once our coughing had subsided, the lethal chili pepper oil was added and blended into a smooth paste. This concoction might not make the recipe pages of "Fine Cuisine," but for anyone with an iron-lined stomach and bravery to match, we deemed it a delicacy.

We did not stand on ceremony or presentation: the tortilla chips were spread directly on the counter and the eating began. Restraint was difficult: we were starving and as fast I eat, Jamo was a contender—his index finger always the first to indelicately scrape the last remnants from the bowl and ensure every last ounce of guacamole was eaten.

Keeping up with each other required concentration and persistence, and the beer and whiskey never tasted so good as after a hard day of fishing—not to mention successfully returning with all our fingers and toes intact. Occasionally we would mix hors d'oeuvres up with smoked salmon that I had made, or salmon pate', but in truth the chips and guacamole became the standard early on. Variety took a back seat to favorites.

Despite our boorish manners when it came to eating and scratching, early on we assented to a verbal pact: just because we were in the wilderness without any of the gentler sex around to keep us in line, we needed to follow basic Ms. Manner's protocol. All requests began with "please" followed by "thank you" and "you are welcome." It was a rule of civility rarely if ever broken. Jamo was the Sgt. At Arms when it came to enforcement. Quick and stern admonishments followed if protocol wasn't followed.

Other routines departed from the norm. For instance our fishing day was not entirely conventional. Fishermen notoriously attack the waters by the first light of day, arising before the cock crows and daylight has begun in order to be the first on the river. This early morning strategy evaded us. Our days began somewhat later—in part due to fishing late each evening and returning as the sun was setting.

By day two of the trip, if not earlier, we were settled into our regimen. The first one up made coffee, others were served...often while still in bed. Slow awakening eventually led to gear preparation and then breakfast. Cleanup and preparation of lunches followed, and we were out the door by the crack of noon, just in time for the afternoon bite.

Our late departures did not inhibit our fishing though. Summers in Alaska allow for late night excursions when it is still light, and we generally took full advantage of this. It was a rare evening when we were back at the cabin by 8 p.m. and more often we arrived closer to midnight. This made for late dinners, of course, always preceded by a toast to staying alive and good fishing (no matter the catching), and once we could get past the choking fumes of the pepper oil, consumption of our fiery guacamole and chips.

Our cycle was a law of diminishing returns: the later we returned—the later we slept—the later we headed out to fish, the later—you get the picture. I can't honestly say that each of us approached the schedule in the same manner, though.

Jack has never owned a watch—a point of personal pride if not habitual tardiness. He is a businessman with a busy schedule, but being on time falls into the Latino definition—

mas o menos. If you asked him he would say he is always on time, but only by his interpretation.

Even though he may pay little attention to the clock, Jack is a "Nazi" fisherman—at least that's how I describe it. I know of no one who loves to fish more than he does. And he is usually the reason we fish so late. He can't stop himself.

It is bad enough when the fishing is slow—he'll keep at it just so he can catch something. It is worse when the fishing is good: he is a pig in mud. Flying home in the dark, risking life and limb, going hungry...those are all secondary to catching fish.

Most of the time Jamo and I arrive back at the plane from wherever we have been separately flogging the waters at about the same time. My query as to Jack's whereabouts always elicits a similar reply, "He's up the river at that last hole—he had a nice one on when I went by him." This is bad news since Jack will not quit if he is catching anything.

If he is in earshot, we'll start yelling about the lateness of the hour, dinner and the cabin waiting, etc. –all to no avail. There is usually only one way we can pull him off a river, and I can't say for sure that it really works, but at least it gets his attention. We start yelling "Whiskey." Fortunately for us, sometimes his appreciation for a gentlemanly drink will override his preoccupation with catching fish, and he will soon appear in the distance, casting into every eddy and possible fish hideout as he leisurely makes his way to the plane.

Jack is not a heavy drinker, but he appreciates blended Canadian whiskeys, even if he does drink the cheap stuff: R & R. Jamo conversely favors American bourbon—Jack Daniels— and for a while it **had** to be Gentleman Jack (a "top shelf" choice he claims was made by Jack and me to improve his tastes even though I remember the switch at his request) but he eventually conceded that the less expensive Jack Daniels had more flavor, and we switched back to the more plebian version. Keeping the pilot pleased was always our goal.

Every day when we leave the cabin, we haul our emergency supplies to the plane: sleeping bags, extra clothes, tent, freeze dried food, and an emergency supply of whiskey. One rule we never broke was the "8 hours—bottle to throttle" rule, but just in case, there was always an emergency ration of whiskey if we were stranded. This was used on more than one occasion when we would get weathered in and be forced to spend the night on a gravel bar or lake shore. Circumstances beyond our control were no reason to go without a gentlemanly drink—never consumed in excess.

Initially, the only emergency whiskey on board was one or the other: Canadian or bourbon, but not both—probably as a token weight saving gesture. This would invariably initiate the argument of whose booze was better. In 25 plus years, neither party ever gave an inch.

"Jesus, Jack. How can you drink that shit?" Jamo would on rare occasions take a sip to remind himself how horrible Canadian whiskey was. Both swore that they would never actually drink the other's choice of rot gut, but truth be told, that was a huge lie only to be lived on rare occasions. As a result, a vessel of each type became the status quo.

I was never much of a whiskey drinker, but it didn't prevent me from imbibing my fair share of spirits. At first Jamo relented and transported beer to the cabin, which I rationed carefully. The only distilled spirits I could honestly say I enjoyed was gin, but not without tonic mix. This is somewhat of a fu-fu drink when your partners are drinking manly whiskey, but despite occasional disparagement, I didn't take too much flak. The problem wasn't the gin...it was the tonic. Transporting any liquid in a plane other than gasoline or whiskey is treading on risky turf. It is unnecessary weight and increases drag and the forces of gravity. So the pilot always eyed my liter bottles of tonic mix just a little suspiciously as we initially loaded our gear for the long flight. Any extra weight only added to our potential peril and inaugurated oft-repeated lectures. Despite this, Jamo good-naturedly loaded my tonic mixers into the plane with little derogatory comment at the outset of our trips. He seemed more concerned with Jack's two dozen or so fishing poles (by his count) jammed into the plane.

9

The Flight

During the early years we packed the plane to the limit and obviously survived each and every flight, but not without enduring a ton of the previously discussed bitching from the pilot. When the plane had its first engine failure, thankfully without me in it, and AP mechanics later installed a new engine, we began to hear about things other than dying in a fiery crash although that was always at the heart of the argument.

The excess weight caused extra engine strain, which caused wear and tear, which caused excess money. Ultimately, it could result in engine failure, which could cause an untimely death. In my narcissistic view the last part was the most important and any death involving me would be untimely.

Emergency landings were not uncommon on the long flight to and from the area. Typically they were weather related and rather than risk flying into the danger, we would cautiously land on a river somewhere and wait out the rain and clouds. This always caused a certain amount of heartburn—for two reasons. First—it delayed the trip, and secondly—landing and taking off were always the riskiest parts of flying. Landing in an unknown section of river with sometimes swift and tricky currents and who-knows-what lying beneath the surface kept us alert.

On a few occasions, we would erect the tent with the possibility of spending the night or at least camping out until the weather improved. Good camping spots were not always available, and just finding a place to tie up the plane could be a challenge. An overloaded plane stuffed to the gills with gear only added to the potential danger.

That was when we started making two trips...well, not exactly "we"—Jamo made two trips—a pre-trip alone to ferry essential supplies, and a second trip with us. Truth be told, part of the problem was Jamo's diet.

Jamo has an eating disorder. More directly, once he starts eating he can't stop—at least with certain foods. He has never been "fat" and really, during his heavier years, I would probably categorize him as just a wee bit portly. He carried his weight well in his 5'10" frame, and though at that time he appeared somewhat soft in physique, make no mistake—he was as tough as anyone in the outdoors. His tendency to eat nonstop never slowed his activity level, but he seemed self-conscious about his weight and the resulting health implications.

Jamo also struggled with a rare form of arthritis which required some offbeat remedies at times, so Jack and I as purveyors of the food for the trip would each year cater to some dietary mumbo jumbo to make him feel good about himself. He forbade Jack's wife Carol from making chocolate chip cookies, for instance, because Jamo would have the entire box gone within 24 hours of arriving at the cabin. Dietary supplements included raspberry tealeaves among other things. Instructions were clear—make sure these magical potions were included. Dietary selections had to be followed to a T. Again, I didn't always listen to the rationale; it was simply easier to go along.

It was fine with us...we would do our best to accommodate whatever he wanted. After all let's be honest, he was providing the cabin and the plane, not to mention paying for the gas. The first year I accompanied them, the expectation was that we would split the gas, but at the end of the trip Jamo magnanimously said we could get the food and drink and he'd cover the gas...a great deal for us. Therefore we were willing to buy whatever he wanted...steaks every night...fillet mignon...but wait...there was the issue of weight—not his—but that of transported goods—even food. So in order to fly safely (and for Jamo to get in some extra flying and fishing by himself, no doubt), he started making a "pre-trip." This led to another luxury that soon became part of our routine: wine.

I had been a wine drinker for some time and had even gone so far as to join the ranks of effete wine snobbery by taking oenology classes where we used words like nose and legs—not to describe body parts—but the qualities of the drink. Admittedly, I was a bit of a Philistine in that highbrow crowd, but nonetheless, I gradually acquired a modicum of knowledge about grapes and their by-products and could espouse the drink with semi appropriate adjectives regarding texture, smell, and taste.

So when Jamo became a wine drinker, transporting bottles of the beverage to the cabin suddenly became a priority and I did not argue, far preferring a tasty cabernet sauvignon to other forms of alcohol to accompany a well earned meal at the end of a hard day of fishing and tramping through the tundra. Of course true wine snobs cannot simply drink wine...it must be discussed, Jamo argued, and so early on the cabin acquired a "flavor wheel" which neatly listed all the adjectives about wine that we unpolished fishermen could never conjure on our own. As the oenophile with the most experience, it was not long before blind taste tests became a natural consequence of this progression...me being the blind subject who had to discern the difference between zinfandels, cabs, pinot noirs, and various blends.

Naturally the goal was to prove me the fool: nothing really too extraordinarily difficult, but pride being what it is and courting disaster, I boasted I should be able to tell the difference. As an attorney, Jamo was comfortable using deceit. I could and should expect anything, and we needed corroborating witnesses to ensure there would be no skullduggery. The outcome as I remember, though eyewitness accounts may differ, was that I got most of them right but eventually stumbled over a cheap pinot noir.

In the end I had to endure at least 10 years of humiliation for my faux pas. No bother, Jamo would have pressed me until I failed anyway—I just saved him time and did it earlier rather than later. In his repeated attempts to test my taste, he would occasionally give me different glasses of the same wine, or use similar tactics in an effort to trip me up—all this because I was the only one who could name the four "noble" grapes, basic memorization that failed Jack for several years despite his ability to do complex mathematical calculations in his head.

But really, the bottom line was that we were, in fact, now transporting heavy glass bottles of wine by floatplane nearly 500 miles to a remote cabin. This flew in the face of previous trips where we had been admonished about carrying too many fly rods. The change to wine drinking only occurred when Jamo started making the pre-trip trip. Of course this also created the excuse to really pack all kinds of non-essential items, but we were reminded that there were never any guarantees that we would actually make it to the cabin due to various and sundry things that could go wrong, so no perishables or items critical to our survival could go on the pre-trip.

It really was more of an excuse for Jamo to get in a little solo fishing, I think, but he would never admit that. All we heard were stories of his personal sacrifice for our wellbeing. We were told only scant stories of his successes fishing on these pre-trips. Instead Jamo would continually remind us how he was potentially sacrificing life and limb for our ultimate comfort. Sainthood for him was an eventual certainty.

10

The Kellys Come to Dillingham

Jimmy and Mike Kelly

In some 25 years of making this annual pilgrimage, various events tend to run together, and time has a way of distorting truth. The witnesses to my lack of oenophilic expertise, in addition to Jack, happened to be a father/son duo—Mike Kelly and his teenage son Jimmy. The three of us—Jamo, Jack, and I—had been coming to the cabin for some years, but one year, probably in the early 90's, Jamo announced he was inviting the Kellys. Mike Kelly was a skilled pilot, and Jamo had known him professionally during Jamo's tenure as chief attorney for the University of Alaska. Jimmy was just out of high school as I recall that trip, and we watched him grow up through the course of several other trips over the years to the cabin. The addition of new members to our fraternity required logistical juggling and coordination so that none of our firmly established habits, both dietary and drink-wise, would be negatively impacted. It also required modifications to our fishing routines so we could accommodate two airplanes instead of one. To coordinate our efforts Jamo asked me to hook up with them via email and send them our basic menu requirements.

Mike and Jimmy were scheduled to arrive a few days after us. We had set up the cabin, completed some preliminary scouting and fishing, and awaited their arrival on the due date. It was probably July because that part of Alaska was starting to get dark at night around 10 p.m. or so, and landing at night on an unlit lake was something we tried to avoid. Nevertheless, that night as we sat in the cabin looking across the lake at the mountains it became evident that if they were going to make it on their appointed date, they would be landing in the dark. In fact, when we heard the plane overhead, it was pitch black. Jamo instantly knew it was Mike's plane...no one else would be flying that late, and sure enough, we heard him touch down and soon the Cessna's bright headlights came into view as it taxied around the point of the island.

After they beached and tied down the plane, we helped unload their gear and ferry it to the cabin, and the first thing Jack and I noted was that they could put us to shame when it came to flying heavy. In fairness, only two souls on board make a huge difference in a plane's weight carrying capacity. Mike is a big guy but Jimmy probably only stepped on the scale at 155 pounds at the time. Nonetheless, their load was impressive. They left nothing behind it seemed. As we carried the endless boxes up to the cabin, Jack wondered aloud, "Jesus, Jamo, why can't we bring this kind of stuff?"

As previously stated, I had never met the Kellys except by email. Since we had been making the trip for years, we were so set in our ways that it was primarily a matter of them just adding to meals that we had already planned. The bonus, though, was that they brought heavy things only imagined by us: real potatoes, apples and oranges, fresh produce including tomatoes, and vegetables. Opening their boxes was like Christmas—with one exception: their wine selection was clearly substandard. Jack, who barely touched wine, may not have realized the import of this deed, but Jamo and I exchanged wary glances. This could be serious.

Once the plane was unloaded, we toasted and proceeded to hear about their trip. The flight from Fairbanks to the cabin is relatively straight forward, unless you care about dying. Much of the flying happens through vast open valleys and flat space, mostly uninhabited, but hills and mountains are always present. Weather reports are sketchy at best and therefore weather is always an unknown factor: low clouds can create huge visibility problems for the route we choose and detours use valuable gas which is always tight.

Initially our navigation was strictly by conventional means: a map and a compass. Because we were flying under visual rules—VFR— we were always on the earth side of any existing clouds. Rarely did we fly above 1000 feet and the disadvantage of that is the limited perspective it provides for mapping a route. Blue skies and altitude make visibility a breeze, but low-level flying makes all the landmarks look frighteningly the same as the mountaintops are cut off and perspectives are distorted. Eventually I became the navigator when I moved to the jump seat, a job I took very seriously carefully plotting each leg of the trip on the map and comparing it to the mountains and rivers around us as we proceeded.

While I had some flying experience in small planes, most of this was new to me, and Jamo was a good teacher, always explaining, testing, correcting. One of the problems with a trip like this is that the areas we are flying over are remote; weather prediction is mainly what you see in front of you. We knew from the map that the final leg of our route involves flying over a series of gradually rising hills that form the headwaters of the Nushagak drainage system which eventually flows into Bristol Bay. Once over that series of low mountains, it is pretty much a downhill flight with water and flat tundra underneath for emergency landings. This offers at least a modicum of security, plus once we see the Nushagak River, it is a fairly short trip to the upper lakes and ample space to land a floatplane if necessary.

The problem is that these hilltops sneak up on you, and we needed 1000 feet minimum to get over them. The "pass," such as it is, is actually unnamed and unmarked except by Jamo's plotted route. It is really just a slightly lower section of hills that look basically like all the others around them, but once safely behind us, leads directly into the Nushagak. Cloud cover is common on our route, so the margin of error is not huge and as a result, it can be confining. I cannot imagine doing any part of this trip in the dark as the Kelly's did.

The pass is about an hour from the cabin and if the moon is bright and skies are clear, it is probably no big deal, no matter the hour. Despite these reassurances, I personally prefer flying with sunglasses in bright daylight. Mike Kelly had tons of experience flying in Alaska and commercial ratings to boot. It was clear to both Jack and me that Jamo respected his flying skills greatly, so when he touched down we were somewhat shocked by the lateness of their arrival. However, over the years this proved to be an oft-repeated pattern.

Mike was then the CEO of our local electrical cooperative. He was nearing retirement and as a highly respected member of the community, he served on many boards and commissions. It is also probably safe to say that his political views were 180 degrees opposite of mine. This was not really an issue—politically we were diverse as it was. Jamo had retired from the family law firm to become chief attorney for the university, but his previous practice was as a personal injury lawyer. Not to stereotype, but by nature he tended to be fairly liberal in his viewpoint as well. Jack, a registered Republican, occasionally attended political gatherings, but he did not wear his political views on his sleeve: he was fairly low key about politics in general and seemed to have an open mind when it came to political discussions. Politics was not a topic we discussed much, not because we didn't have opinions, but fishing was really the priority. Political discussions typically only occurred when weather forced us to stay in the cabin, and even then they were rare.

As a teacher, union member, spouse of a social worker, I was pretty much the standard bearer for liberalism in the group although, again, Jamo and I pretty much thought alike about politics. Admittedly I rarely if ever voted Republican, so I guess that defines the bottom line no matter how open-minded I professed to be. Politics, though, only seemed to creep in on the edges of our conversations. When we weren't talking about fishing, we were heaping verbal feces on one another.

This is good because Mike was a dyed in the wool conservative Republican. Alaskan politics have always been strange, and, in fact, they seem to get stranger by the year. There was little about politics that we could probably discuss with any consensus with the Kellys there. All of us knew better than to force the issue, though, so conversation tended to be more banter than anything else. Mike's oft repeated slanders regarding unions and liberals were generally ignored. My tongue bore the brunt of my reserved opinions, and I bit it constantly.

Both Mike and Jamo consider themselves as raconteurs. They know how to spin a story, and each one obviously prides himself in that skill. In fact, for many years we were lulled to sleep by Jamo's bedtime recitation of various Robert Service poems, especially "The Shooting of Dan McGrew," which was impressive just for remembering all the words with appropriate inflection if for no other reason.

His father, Bob Parrish, was an obvious source of admiration as well as the source of many of Jamo's stories. Bob Parrish grew up in West Virginia where story telling was an art form. I knew of Bob only by reputation even though I had been around him many times growing up on the ski slopes where he was a fixture. His influence on the family was profound (four of his five boys followed suit and became attorneys in the family law firm) and Jamo's retelling of his father's stories would never fail to keep Jack and me in stitches. Over the years, we could recite the punch lines of nearly every story (retold regularly) in advance, but they were always appreciated, regardless.

So when Mike and Jimmy arrived it was almost like a battle of the wits. No comment went unnoticed. Heaven help anyone who made a verbal faux pas: criticism rained on slip-ups and mistakes of any kind. The awkwardness of new comrades in camp soon disappeared and gave way to self-defense mechanisms. Mike invariably attributed any mistake I made— breaking an egg yolk, over or under cooking someone's bacon, losing a fish— to my liberal leaning philosophy. This was clearly not a camp for the weak of heart. Thank God Jimmy was there to take much of the heat off the rest of us.

Mike and Jimmy have a father-son relationship to be admired. A clear, unabashed love and respect existed between the two of them. Jimmy, despite his young age was skilled in many ways, and he jumped right in to help out at every turn—and rarely at Mike's urging. His energy was infectious if not tiring to watch. The Howdy Doody smile never left his face, and while many of the nuances of our conversation were initially over his head, he always joined in the laughter—even when he was the butt of the joke.

Jimmy could cook...a valuable asset for one so young. And he did not scrimp on ingredients—fresh tomatoes, fruit, produce...all willingly shared. His public service was beyond reproach. When a glass was empty he filled it. When the coffee pot was drained he made more. He jumped right in to do dishes. He was a whirling dervish of youthful energy. He had a downside though.

While our wine list did not include top shelf Bordeaux or expensive cabs, they were reasonable varietals in the $10-12 range—inexpensive but good, at least to our basic tastes. Jimmy poured our wine like water. The wine they brought that first trip was clearly of a lower caliber, but more importantly, it all seemed to be disappearing much too quickly...which in fact was the case.

This was compounded by some inclement weather that forced us to stay at the cabin. Low-pressure systems frequent the area, and our visual reference for flying is the mountaintop across the lake from the cabin. When we can't see it, we stay put. If we couldn't fly, we couldn't fish, and so we passed time by reading, eating, card playing, and staring out the window trying to make the clouds disappear. As the magical 5 o'clock hour approached, thoughts drifted to other things, and once the first person poured a drink, thoughts of fishing vanished. But out of sympathy for the bottle to throttle rule, no one drank unless the pilot gave the word that flying was out for the day.

Dan Gavora, the owner of the cabin a couple of hundred yards to the west of us on the island, had joined us as well for meals that trip since the weather also prevented his departure back to Fairbanks in his plane. With his addition at dinner and evening festivities combined with Jimmy's heavy handed pouring, it was only a matter of time before we ran out of sauce, which we did. But Dan had a boat and a vehicle at the landing three miles away, and a mercy trip could be made into Dillingham, a 20-mile drive from the landing where essentials could be purchased. Which is exactly what happened—and soon we were flush again—except the reinforcements came in boxes, probably because it was the only option available in the town.

It was one thing to readjust our tastes to the lower dominions of the Kelly wine, but an entirely different thing to have only box wine to drink. Admittedly, these wines have improved over time although I'm not sure I can verify that from personal experience...but rumor has it. Back in the early 90's though, these wines left most of the quality outside the box. They were deemed marginally drinkable under our somewhat dire situation.

However, dreadful circumstances call for drastic measures, and to the best of my knowledge we politely forced down a portion of the stuff before eventually declaring it not worth our time, most likely after Dan had departed to avoid insult. As a footnote however, to Mike and Jimmy's credit—in future trips they always came overstocked with excellent wines. Lesson learned. The eventual verbal retribution (mainly from Jamo who's mouth knows no filter in fish camp) contributed to the improvement in wine selection after that, and Jimmy became a skilled sommelier of sorts—well ahead of his time.

11

Jimmy Becomes a Foil

From the first trip, the unbroken rule of the cabin necessitated that doors remain open so that brisk fresh air for sleeping could easily enter unless and until snow was falling. The weather at the cabin, often cool in the 50's, could be warm on occasion, even by lower 48 standards, and the upstairs sleeping arrangement combined with the laws of thermal energy ensured that if any part of the cabin were stuffy, it would be where we slept. Anyone complaining about open doors felt the full brunt of Jamo's wrath. His remarks on the subject were always bookended with profanity...that's how strongly he felt about it. The first morning after Mike and Jimmy arrived, Jimmy received a dose of that venom.

I don't recall if it started with an innocuous verbal plea about the temperature, or if in fact Jimmy actually tried to build a fire in the wood stove, but like a hand on a hot burner, he felt the sting of Jamo's wrath when he complained about the cold cabin.

"Jesus Christ, put on a jacket for God's sake. We're not building any fucking fire."

Point made.

Jimmy, being somewhat naïve, however, would occasionally return to the subject. He just couldn't get it through his puppy-dog head that anyone would willingly freeze to death when a perfectly good, albeit somewhat rusted stove, sat idly waiting for a fire to be lit. His pleas grew first into minor begging, but after a while he just did it to push Jamo's buttons, I think. If so, it never failed to work. Words that would cause an ironworker to blush punctuated Jamo's response each time.

Jimmy's inclusion in the group, though, was a sort of serendipity for us. He and I struck it right off. As a teacher and coach, I had known him indirectly when as a middle school student his Monroe Catholic team beat my 7th graders for the district basketball championship. He liked to smoke an occasional cigar, and the two of us would share stories about our sporting seasons on the porch while smoking a stogie. But the real benefit was that he took a major amount of the criticism from Jamo, who could lay it on pretty heavy. It was never truly mean spirited, but you had to have a thick skin to survive. Sarcasm and criticism went hand in hand and so Jack and I, but especially I—prospered with the advent of Jimmy since Jamo's wrath and wit were redirected at him. He was like a puppy that kept stepping on his own ears to everyone's delight; and his grin never diminished.

Jimmy had no adult filters. He happily stated whatever was on his mind, and for his age his insight seemed refreshing. But like most his age, his worldview was a bit naïve, especially when compared to a crowd of curmudgeons. He did know a thing or two about fishing, and when we finally did get out of the cabin and hit the streams, his screams of delight couldn't help but put a smile on your face...that is, unless he was catching all the fish. Never forget that fishermen are pigs, and competition, though unstated, is omnipresent among men and especially fishermen.

Mike was clearly in 7th heaven with his son by his side and his pride was evident in play-by-play summations. I don't think Mike really cared if he personally caught fish or not—as long as Jimmy was doing so. So for us the diversion of company at the cabin was a pleasant enough experience, but I'd be lying if I said we weren't just a little happy when we had the place all to ourselves again. This is not because of any negativity: it is just that the logistics of five are more complicated than three. By the time the Kelly's first joined us, we had our routines down to a science. It was the kind of comfort that comes from an old sweatshirt: you know where all the holes and stains are, but that just makes it better—there are no worries about ruining it.

12

The Competition Begins

When Mike and Jimmy were with us, it necessitated that we fish places that could accommodate two airplanes instead of one. Most of the time this was no big deal, but occasionally it was tight to get two planes with 35-foot wingspans maneuvered up the mouth of a stream or in a good place to tie off.

This was illustrated on one occasion when we decided to fish a small stream on the north side of Lake Beverly. The mouth of the creek where it met the lake was a deep channel with dense brush on the channel side and a shallow gravel bar opposite. We would avoid the shallow gravel bar and taxi up the eastern bank and into the stream, carefully avoiding damaging the wing on the willows and alder along the river's edge. Jack and I would jump off the float onto the shore—rope in hand—and tie the plane off. The river channel was probably at least 6 feet deep in this part and on a cut bank, so stepping into the water was not an option.

With the arrival of the Kellys, parking became an issue, so Jamo decided to taxi as far as possible upstream to make room for Mike's plane in the tight space available. The river soon narrowed appreciably into a typical shallow creek that was not navigable but still held some nice fish if we stealthily sneaked up on them, walking along the bank and through the brush on a narrow animal trail.

Jamo instructed Jack and me to stand on the float near the bank—each with a rope at the ready—and he would taxi as far upstream as possible. We were to watch the channel and bark orders as needed to avoid grounding the plane and hitting the brush with the wing tip. Jamo's head projected from the opposite side window as he tried to hear our commands while the big engine loudly taxied us upriver.

I was in a precarious position on the rear of the float, ready to hook a loop over the cleat before jumping off onto the shore and securing the plane, rear end first, to the bank. The problem was that Jamo was paying attention to Jack near the front of the plane and unable to see or hear me.

As we slowly made our way upstream, I could see thick alders sweeping under the wing and steadily coming my way. I yelled to both Jamo and Jack to steer left into the stream, but my pleas went unnoticed and unheeded. Like a slow motion picture, I watched as the heavy branches progressed my way with no escape in sight. I inched to the extreme rear edge of the pontoon next to the water rudders as the danger crept ever closer, my fate seemingly a certainty.

Finally I screamed as loud as I could at Jamo—still oblivious to my plight—to turn so the tail spun away from the branches. Mike and Jimmy, downstream from us and now out of their plane, watched as the scene unfolded. The thick limbs finally reached my precarious perch and slowly and methodically swept me into the deep channel.

Up to my neck in water and feet groping for any kind of purchase, I grabbed onto the rear cleat of the pontoon. By now Jack realized, too late, what was happening and waved to Jamo to kill the engine.

No matter, all could now hear my cussing and swearing as I clung to the float, my entire body immersed in the chilly water. My feet were a long ways from touching bottom.

Jamo was the main target of my epithets, although I'm sure I included others and their relatives as I struggled to pull my waterlogged carcass out of the creek. Jimmy rushed up the bank and helped drag me out of the water. By now the plane had moved beyond the offending branches and I was able to haul myself onto the float with Jimmy's aid. My waders had filled with water despite the belt designed to restrict the flow inside them.

I cooled off literally and figuratively in a few moments as I peeled off my soaking clothes, wrung out my polypro jacket, and got into my dry emergency clothing. Jamo wore an embarrassed look of concern for an appropriate amount of time before commencing with the normal doses of grief he regularly dispensed on anyone within earshot.

This was the only time I ever unwittingly went in the drink over the years and it served to illustrate several lessons, not the least of which pointed out the difficulty of parking planes in some of our favorite spots. So to avoid these issues, we regularly relied on other vessels to get to the good spots.

Each party had an inflatable boat packed in the plane for navigating rivers—Jamo's was a Metzeler 4 man raft with a 15-horse Johnson outboard that we mounted to the transom. The M.O. was always to motor upstream and float downstream—a hard and fast rule that we only violated one time, nearly to our peril, but that is another story. The rationale was that if we encountered engine problems with the outboard, we could always float back to the plane. Paddling upstream against the current was not really an option.

The boat allowed us access to incredible areas gained no other way. The plane got us in the proximity of good fishing, but the inflatable literally took us to the fish. Originally, in our early trips we simply ran rivers that were deep enough for the outboard, but in reality we were constantly hitting rocks in the shallow spots that chewed the prop to pieces. Jamo is all about speed when it comes to boating, and to be fair, getting the boat on step was the only way to avoid many of the pitfalls awaiting us in the shallower sections of the rivers. As a result we typically raced at full throttle whenever possible, Jack and me screaming and hanging on for dear life as Jamo whipped the tiller back and forth, avoiding boulders and navigating into the deeper channels.

The discoveries of potentially great fishing spots usually occurred first from the plane, and we would strategize a way to get to them from the closest body of water where we could land—or more importantly, take off—without undue jeopardy to life and limb. Invariably these exploratory trips ended in a great deal of pushing and pulling the boat against the swift currents over logjams and riffles, through thick brush, and over beaver dams, much of the time with Jamo still sitting in the boat barking orders.

On numerous occasions we marveled in retrospect at the places we were able to go in this fashion, mostly by sheer willpower, not to mention muscle power. The original fifteen horse motor more than adequately propelled the three of us upriver as long as the prop was intact and not chewing granite, but for security, we always carried extra cotter pins, a file for "speed-tuning" the prop, an extra prop, and, of course, electrical tape. And while serious motor problems rarely occurred, we were always aware that our fate could turn on a dime with a boat blowout or some similar catastrophe miles from the plane.

The Kellys carried a 4 man Zodiac with the traditional foot-pump to inflate it. Our inaugural boat trip with them accompanying us set the stage for future adventures. Jamo is as competitive as anyone I know, and as we landed in the lake and taxied to shore where we would put the boats together, he reminded us, "We have got to kick their ass. You guys take care of the plane and I'll unload the boat and motor."

Pumping up the Zodiac the old fashioned way

As nonchalantly as possible but going as fast as we could, we were out to impress. Every move had a purpose as we emulated an efficient racing team. Jack and I first tied down the plane while Jamo emptied it of our gear. Then Jack and I proceeded to inflate the boat with our secret weapon.

Jamo had rigged a most likely illegal apparatus to the battery of the airplane: an Italian hair blower with a 20 foot or so extension cord wired to it so it would reach the boat from the plane. The end of the blower had a plastic fitting taped to the dryer with (what else?) electrical tape, which perfectly fit into the air valves in the inflatable. He had selected an Italian hair dryer not because of any cultural advantage but because it was the only one found that was 24 volt, a requirement of the plane's electrical system. This device was a godsend; it saved us countless hours of sweaty hand pumping over the years, but more importantly, it was fast.

Once the hair dryer had inflated a compartment to capacity, we still had to pump the raft to the appropriate pressure. A traditional hand pump completed the process, and even though much of the hard part had taken place with electricity, finishing off the raft on a hot day was a short but arduous activity which Jack and I shared, trading off as needed. No hands stood idle; we were all three unloading, loading, attaching the seat, mounting the motor, and attaching the fuel line. In roughly 10 minutes we were pumped up and primed for fishing. The Kellys stood stonily; methodically standing in place, hands on hips, one boot going up and down on the foot pump, watching air slowly fill their raft one puff at a time. But our victory was short lived.

As I said, when motoring up or down the rivers we were always in danger of damaging the prop on rocks, riffles, boulders, anything lurking below the surface. In the old days before jet units became commonplace, riverboats in Alaska were typically equipped with an engine "lift." The entire motor mount could move up or down, controlled by a long handle next to the driver that leveraged the heavy engine. Whenever an obstacle like a riffle approached, the handle could be pushed down, raising the motor so the prop skimmed over the obstruction. It was easy and efficient, and until jet units obviated them, they were ubiquitous in Alaskan rivers.

Mike had crafted a lift for his inflatable that did exactly the same thing. So with just Jimmy and Mike in their Zodiac, and with a lift at their disposal, they fairly flew up the river. We, on the other hand, had three of us in the boat, more gear, and no lift. When we came to a shallow spot, we either tried to go around it or grind through it. Neither ploy was usually successful, and when the motor flew out of the water, chunks of metal suddenly missing or reformed at new angles, both Jack and I would bail out and start pulling the boat against the current. Mike and Jimmy sailed past us, unscathed, still seated, and grins beaming.

You can bet that if someone has a bigger, better, or especially faster product, Jamo will do what he can to get it, and that is precisely what happened for the following year.

Of Jamo's four brothers, three are attorneys. Dan, however, became a pipefitter and a professional welder. Dan knows boats, motors, and most things that go fast, and so at Jamo's urging he copied the Kelly's design and built an adjustable motor mount out of lightweight aluminum that worked perfectly on the inflatable. This improvement allowed us to travel to new places with greater speed and with less effort.

The boat-plane combination gave us access to some great fishing, but certainly, the plane was the keystone: it could take us long distances to remote streams where we would encounter few, if any, fishermen. All we needed was a stretch of water long enough to land and take off. Once the plane was down and secured, we could travel upriver in the inflatable to get to truly remote spots or travel up small streams unfrequented by guides.

The reality, unfortunately, is that these places are truly few and far between, even in remote Alaska—the lodges have riverboats with high powered motors and jet units that can go anywhere we can go and then some. They stash boats around the countryside and it is simply a matter of setting up semi-permanent tent camps for the guides and flying the clients in and out. This allows them to utilize large stretches of river, and effectively few places exist where they cannot go. This only gave us greater incentive to find new fishing holes away from other fishermen.

13

Catch and Release

When I began this story, I commented on the surprise I felt when told that the fish were released. Killing fish was part of the process for me growing up. I'm sure I felt some reluctance when, as a young boy fishing with my father, I was told to kill the fish I had caught. It was the humane thing to do—bonk them on the head with a make shift club and give them a quick death. Of course it was really never that quick. They squirmed, gurgled, flopped, and eventually suffered a fish version of a death throe before finally lying still.

We would place them in the wicker creel with some wet grass, and periodically dip the whole basket into the water to keep them fresh. Repeated applications of this process undoubtedly inured me after a time. I think, too, that the general understanding of most fishermen, true or not, is that fish don't feel pain. Either way, I now see no reason to kill fish unless they are to provide an immediate meal, salmon being the notable exception since they are about to die anyway and they store nicely in our freezer over the winter.

This naturally raises the question about the ethics of sport fishing, and without getting too philosophical, we do our best to release fish in as safe a manner as possible. Most of the time we free them without touching them. Jamo was a master at releasing fish, and I did my best to emulate him, grabbing the fly carefully between thumb and first finger and giving it a quick jerk inward to release the debarbed hook without grabbing the fish while it is still in the water. The fact that they invariably dart back to the depths seems to imply they will survive.

I'm also a realist. While my wife avoids beef products, I have no problem eating most any kind of meat including aquatic varieties. I do think animals should be treated ethically, but then the discussion is in the definition of just what that means. PETA and I have little to discuss due to what I consider their over-the-top excesses. In short, though, we do our best to fish ethically and responsibly.

But occasionally we would keep fish for a meal. Sometimes a fish would take a fly too deeply and cause a mortal wound necessitating keeping it, and other times fish mortality was intentional and pre-planned. One such occurrence took place at a small stream flowing into Lake Nerka—Lynx Creek. Lynx Creek is a tiny rivulet that flows out of Lynx Lake, a mountain lake probably ½ mile long and just big enough for a safe takeoff. We used to stop there frequently and fish the outflow of the lake since the flight home often passed over the area. The stream is classic rainbow water: it twists and turns down the hillside through brush, spruce, and cottonwood, moving swiftly around boulders and logs until it eventually disappears into the forest for its 1-2 mile trip to Lake Nerka. After landing we would tie the plane up a ways from the outlet of the lake and hike to the stream down a game trail, practicing stealth fishing.

Initially I was a bit of a clown at this.

"Jesus, could you be any noisier? These guys are wondering what the stampede is all about!" Jamo in a stage whisper was my critic. Or, "Christ, don't let your shadow go over the hole. The big ones are long gone by now." Admittedly, I had no Chippewa blood in my system.

By reputation rainbow trout are extremely alert and watchful, and variations in shadows and movement all put them on high alert which makes fishing difficult at best—at least that is the case if you believe Jamo, and it does make sense. Once we got near the stream, we would hunker down and tread lightly, walking Indian style, low and jockeying for position without destroying the tactical advantage of the others. This resulted in great fishing once we arrived at the creek mouth—size being the only drawback. Here a Lilliputian 6 inch rainbow was a prized catch. These diminutive devils fought like the dickens when hooked, and while they were no match for even the lightest fishing gear, it was fairly embarrassing to brag about the most or the biggest catch. I never failed to proffer the oft-repeated line from television fishing shows in a pseudo Southern drawl, "Nice fish, Bubba," as Jamo reeled in a hearty 5 incher wriggling more like a worm than a rainbow. Each time we fished there we secretly hoped we would stumble on a few lunkers, but the net result was always the same: tiny fingerlings.

On one occasion Jamo talked Jack and me into walking the length of the creek down to Nerka while he would ferry the plane down there and meet us at the lake. We dutifully obeyed, thinking this would be untrod turf and could result in some great fishing further downstream. The size of fish at the upper lake should have been our first clue. But then that wasn't the biggest problem.

The stream wound its way through thick impenetrable willows and alder, and the only place to walk was in the middle of the creek, a task made easy since it never got more than about a foot deep in the deepest holes. Casting was all but impossible...it was more along the lines of flipping the fly ahead a few feet and letting it float downstream before stomping through those waters. Clearly, whoever was in front had the advantage, if that is what you would call it.

A few places looked slightly better as far as fish habitat, but then they also looked great as bear habitat. We knew there were bears around the area: tracks were everywhere, and even though bruins generally stay well away from humans, Jack and I hailed greetings with the traditional, "Hey, bear...hey, bear" all the way down the stream. Quiet courage took a back seat to a noisier form of bravado when push came to shove.

When we got to the bottom after bushwhacking our way, Jamo was standing in Lake Nerka at the mouth of the creek, a traditional dolly hole, having fished out the rainbows in the stream just above where it enters the lake and where there is slightly more flow and 16-18 inchers occasionally lurk. The lake fishing for char/dollies could be fantastic at times and they were decent sized. And if the salmon were in, we would get cheap thrills hooking them and hanging on while they screamed out line down to the backing and occasionally put on aerial displays as they attempted to spit out the fly. Most of the time they were Chums (also called dog salmon if that gives a clue to their popularity—they were often used as dog food in the villages), and even though they are not generally prized for human consumption over other species of salmon, they were typically dime bright and feisty. Even a small salmon is a big fish most of the time.

One particular trip to Lynx Creek stands out as Jamo had decided we would have a grayling feast for dinner. We all grew up eating grayling since they were the predominant fish in the Interior rivers. These beautiful creatures, dark and shiny with their notably tall dorsal fin like a freshwater sailfish, are truly the iconic aquatic representatives of interior and northern Alaska. Any grayling over 18 inches is a huge fish and anything over 20 is a whopper.

Before embarking on this foray, though, we had to listen to Jamo's lecture about the perfect sized grayling for eating. The small ones had it all over the big fish, he reminded us, and also because grayling take forever to get to any bragging size, keeping the babies allowed the medium guys to attain reproductive status. It was good eco system management. So after landing on Lake Nerka and securing the plane, we walked over to the creek mouth.

As already explained, this was the outflow of Lynx Lake, and while the creek was miniscule as it trickled down the brushy hillside through bear country, it widened appreciably toward the bottom where it flattened out into the lake. Nonetheless, it was by any measure still a tiny stream. From time to time we did catch a few nice rainbows at the mouth of the creek where it was deeper and protected by overhanging brush, as well as some big dollies in Lake Nerka at the outflow. Within minutes I had a grayling on, and I prepared to release the behemoth 5-incher wriggling spasmodically for all his life.

"No...that's perfect...keep him," Jamo yelled from downstream.

"You have GOT to be kidding," I replied. "This is like one bite of dinner."

"No, anything bigger is too big...that's perfect. Trust me." His sincerity was moving if not entirely convincing.

Well, after that direction I can safely say that we had a slaughter. The fish fairly fell into our plans (and eventually the frying pan) in a frenzy. The plane handled the extra weight without a whimper: we popped off the water despite the heft of our catch.

Cleaning them was another problem. These fish were too small to gut and scale in the traditional manner, so again following Jamo's instructions, we simply ate them whole, minus their heads, of course. Grayling normally are bony, and eating them requires grabbing the spinal column once they are cooked and lifting the bones out in one clean section. Not to worry with these guys—they were so small we ate them bones, tail and all. If you are thinking sardines...you are on the right track. Despite their miniscule size, we cooked them in the traditional manner, dipping them in Krust-ez and frying them in oil.

The subsequent feast elicited non-stop commentary from Jack and me. Jack is normally a pensive eater, but the event merited culinary criticism from even him, "Gees, Jamo, I feel like a baby killer." Or "What a feast! I don't think I've ever eaten this many grayling at one sitting."

Jamo, unapologetic, bore it all with reserved stoicism and mainly responded with murmurs of delight as he greedily dug in and cleaned his plate. "You guys just won't admit what a feast this is. You have to admit, these are great tasting."

We never replicated the experience despite the haut cuisine we experienced that night. One minnow feed seemed to satisfy our fish appetites for grayling for years to come.

14

Pikers

A frying pan full of 5 inch grayling wasn't the last fish meal we ate over the 25 years or so at the cabin, but it was definitely the most delicate. On another trip we decided to try for another species—a voracious, lightening quick predator that can grow to hefty weight and length—Northern Pike. While halibut is sometimes called "poor man's lobster," a few would take it a step further and pass the compliment on to pike, a fleshy white meat fish prized in northern climes for its size and ravenous appetite.

Pike can be and are caught on flies, but their sharp teeth, which can bite through ordinary tackle, typically require steel leader. They can get to epic size and 20 pounds or even larger fish are fairly common. Not only is their size epic, so are the stories of pike fishing. One friend told me about fishing for pike in a remote lake known as a habitat for huge fish. Sitting out in the middle of the lake in a boat, he and his companion were having a beer and chatting while one of the rod tips hung over the edge of the boat. Suddenly a pike came out of the water, grabbed the "pixie" dangling in mid air over the gunnel, and took off, rod in tow, around the lake. They never retrieved the rod but witnessed one pissed off pike periodically porpoising and doing his best to rid himself of the unwanted appendage. This scenario has been repeated numerous times—if one is wont to believe fish stories.

Jamo had also experienced a similar episode under much the same conditions, but this time his nephew was using his dad's brand new Winston fly rod when a pike grabbed it and took off in similar fashion. The nephew cried in desperation at the thought of losing his dad's prized rod, but the story ended happily when they eventually hooked onto the miles of line pulled out by the fish and retrieved the rod after great effort, minus the fish.

Our adventure with pike was not nearly so dramatic. The end of Lake Beverly had a semi swampy area reputably rife with the species, or so we had been informed. Getting into these areas can be tricky as the lake typically forms long shallows off the shoreline, and having only so much rope, it can be difficult to get a heavy plane close enough to tie off. However, Jack and I got out and pushed the plane toward the shoreline while Jamo sat on the float like an overweight overlord shouting directions, ostensibly because he could see deep water better from the float.

Once tied up, we waded to where we assumed the fish were lurking and got out lightweight spin rods, having no confidence in our fly rods initially. The first thing we did was clip off two of the three hooks on our small pixies, and then squeezed the barb shut on the final hook so we could release the fish easily. Our first casts were immediately met with action as soon as the line was retrieved.

Pike will eat anything, and watching them dart out from the grassy shallows and attack the lures exhilarated each of us. Most often the fish were small—especially for pike—probably 16-20 inches, but hard fighters nonetheless. We caught and released dozens of fish until Jack laid into a nice one later in the afternoon. His Fenwick pack rod bent double, Jack strained to haul the big fish in. Each time he would get it close, the toothy monster would make another run until finally he was dragged in, exhausted. At that point, we decided this would be a good excuse to have a fried Pike dinner. On paper, it sounded like a great idea.

I had never fished for pike before that day, and likewise, to the best of my memory I had never eaten one. Pike are particularly bony, and filleting them is complicated as their bones radiate in several directions, unlike, for instance, a salmon. I'm sure there are Youtube videos explaining the process, but since none were available we relied on Jamo who swore some expertise on the issue. He filleted the fish, and we proceeded to bread it in beer batter and flour and fry it for dinner.

A pike has delicate white meat, and frying it in beer batter seems to be the most common cooking method although I'm sure that culinary experts might argue the point. It was tasty as well as filling. We ate to our hearts content, waddled to the couch almost in unison, and unbeknownst to us at the time, waited for the rumblings to begin.

I'm uncertain who first felt the attack, but in short order we were all running to the outhouse, running being the operative word and not necessarily referencing the movement of feet. Elimination of our feast was a quick process, albeit painful and repeated several times in the course of the evening. We never ascertained the root of the problem, whether the beer batter, the cooking, or the fish, but at that point it made no difference. However, it permanently cured us of eating pike.

15

The Privy

W hich leads to another subject of interest, this one more mundane—the privy. Outhouses, which have mostly disappeared from America, are still ubiquitous in Alaska. Real cabins do not have indoor toilets. In fact, many Alaskan HOMES do not have indoor toilets, at least in rural areas. Indoor conveniences are a true luxury, and the closest thing many people have to an indoor "throne" is a honey bucket, which can be in a heated space or not, but by definition it lacks a flushing mechanism. Just like it sounds (with the exception of the prefix "honey") it is a bucket that is emptied into a cesspool, a hole in the ground, or some place that is, one would hope, sanitary. We did not have a honey bucket.

The cabin at Aleknagik had an outhouse made from 4 sided cedar logs leftover from the original cabin—essentially notched 4x6 timbers. If nothing else, it was hell for stout. It had no door for privacy, but then none was needed. The nearest cabin was nowhere in sight, and the privy was tucked away up the hill from the cabin and surrounded by thick spruce trees and fiddlehead ferns. Privacy was not an issue and the view from the seat was inspiring, an ancillary benefit.

Early in our trips to the cabin, we redesigned the hole cut in the bench where one sat—it had been crudely "chopped" a size too small, and its jagged edges kept your attention during use. A modern toilet seat sat loosely on top of the bench, unfastened, and because it described a hole larger than the hole upon which it sat, alignment over the smaller bench hole was important. The seat could freely slide around which exposed dangerous, potential slivers when misaligned. Without getting too graphic about the details, we eventually enlarged and rounded the bench hole to make our visits slightly less precarious.

Common reading material in the outhouse was an old dated issued of Scientific American, an old "Sailboating" periodical left by someone longing for the sea life, and a Dilbert book, which was dateless and timeless. Any other reading material was apparently deemed too important to stay in the outhouse. Either that or no one was imaginative enough to add to its library over the years. A bucket of lime remained available at all times, so the smells associated with outhouses were limited by frequent application of the white powder. The euphemism around the cabin for a successful bowel movement was that one should not hit the floor unless one was ready to dance. With three of us occupying the premises most of the time, competition for the outhouse was, thankfully, rare. Nonetheless, when the cabin's side door nearest the pathway to the privy suddenly slammed, we knew it was best to wait an appropriate period of time before sending a search party.

Over the years, however, the reception area beneath the seat began to fill dangerously close to the bench—and finally had reached a pinnacle that forced us into action. Jamo, in a pre-trip to the cabin by himself had decided the privy spot had outlived its usefulness and we would be best served by moving the outhouse to virgin territory for a fresh start. This was the project du jour for the trip, and he had started to dig a hole where the new outhouse was to go.

That year was the only year in our many trips without Jack. He had taken his family on a vacation driving around the lower 48, so it was just the two of us with no buffer of any sort for discussion, dinner, or fishing. Jamo showed me the new hole, and indeed, he had started a shallow ditch about 20 feet from the present outhouse, but watching him with a pick and shovel was painful. Unable to bear his inefficient use of the tools, I grabbed them and proceeded to finish digging the hole myself, knowing I could accomplish the job in half the time. Jamo is no stranger to hard work, and once I started, I soon realized why he had not reached China in his digging...the rocky ground required extensive use of a pickaxe for every shovelful gained. I also realized that I had stepped in it, figuratively speaking, and Tom Sawyer would have been proud. Nevertheless, in time I had a hole dug that met Jamo's demanding specifications for length and width, but especially for depth. The pile of rocky soil next to my proud pit gave testimony to my Irish roots. And the hole was deep enough to accommodate years (if not decades) of service.

The outhouse structure then needed to be moved the distance to the new location where it would reside into perpetuity. We knew it would be difficult, and when the two of us tried at first to lift it, it budged not an inch. In fact, we couldn't even tip it. The structure proved to be not only stout, but also exceedingly heavy.

That year our trip overlapped the other group that commonly used the cabin: Jamo's older brother and a couple of attorney friends. Joe, a partner in the cabin, was to arrive at the end of our stay along with Jamo's brother, Nelson, and Jay, a former attorney and at the time a Superior Court judge. I knew Nelson and I had briefly met Jay, but had never laid eyes on Joe. However, by reputation, I knew them all, partly from

Jamo's stories about work, but mainly from stories about their stays in the cabin. They were the complete opposites of us.

Their routine, according to my source, was to leave the cabin bright and early every morning. They ate canned food whenever possible and cereal for breakfast—things quick and easy to fix, and basically they operated far differently than we did. It sounded like they were more successful fishing, at least from Jamo's stories, but then all fishermen are liars so those tales were taken with a salt lick.

As far as I could tell, Jamo, Jack, and I completed most of the cabin's improvements over the years. Somehow, necessary repairs and maintenance always seemed scheduled during our trips, especially projects that were dangerous or difficult. It seemed clear to me that Jamo understood the pecking order— we were the worker bees. Joe provided support by transporting anything heavy to the cabin in his turbo Beaver. And I had no problem with earning my keep. It was part of our dues for using the cabin, and well worth the cost.

So we planned to use good old-fashioned manpower to move the outhouse—that is once Joe, Nelson, and Jay arrived, of course. Surely five of us could do the deed. Except—here we are talking four attorneys and a teacher. Jamo never shied away from hard work, and I'm not saying the others would either. Generally, all four of them were great at giving orders despite the fact that they frequently contradicted one another.

Since Jamo and I had already tried and failed, we knew the task might prove difficult. So we nailed, bolted, and otherwise fastened long 2x4 handles to the sides of the outhouse. We tried to lift it, two men to a side, with Nelson giving orders for the "heave ho." This initial effort immediately snapped the 2x4 handles like toothpicks. Next, we fastened 2x6 pieces of lumber to the edifice, figuring bigger is better.

"Ready now...on three...one, two, threeeeeee."

Nothing. Despite our grunts and groans, the outhouse didn't budge...it was simply too heavy. In the end, we only succeeded in eventually tipping it over.

And that's when the fun began.

With the structure tipped on its back, the hole and its contents previously hidden by the seat of the outhouse were unveiled. The original excavators must have discovered what I had learned in my earlier efforts to dig a pit—the digging was tough! The hole they had dug was only about a foot deep, if that. Once someone had inaugurated it, no one bothered to inspect it for depth, understandably. So for years we had been building a pyramid with a cheap foundation.

Joe, hip boots for protection, jumped in and started shoveling feces into a garbage bag. Jamo, immediately began hauling the bags to my newly dug hole nearby and dumped them. Shit was literally being heaped, but at least it was going into a bag, and Jamo did not utter so much as a complaint while his older brother and Jay provided a non stop barrage of verbiage.

In short order 15 years or so of semi-composted human waste was moved, but Joe continued digging. He was a man on a mission. Nelson, in turn, never stopped his running commentary and instructions, since after all, shoveling shit requires the sarcastic advice of a barrister, while Jay worked his camera non-stop and offered advice of his own. Between Jay and Nelson it was a battle of verbal diarrhea. As much shit as Joe could shovel, it did not come close to the stuff Jay and Nelson were piling on—figuratively, of course.

"Get used to it, boys," I remarked. "I have a hunch this is what eternity looks like for lawyers—standing knee deep in it with a shovel, except the pile never gets smaller." While my remarks fell unappreciated on my audience, I quietly relished my pseudo Stygian Greek metaphor.

By the time we had tipped the outhouse upright and had buried the newly moved contaminant in the other hole, Joe had enlarged the capacity to accommodate a good 25 more years of thoughtful deposits. It was a job well done and he proved his mettle as far as I was concerned. It is the only time I have ever met him, but it is also the kind of experience that sticks with you.

Nailing "handles" to the tipped outhouse

16

Low Lifes

Over the years the cabin was broken into several times. Luckily for me, twice this happened when I was not present. The first break-in occurred the year I had ventured on another trip with friends to Glacier Bay, Alaska, ostensibly commercial fishing for halibut. The halibut haul is another story, but that year Jamo and Jack arrived to find the cabin door open and the cabin, in general, trashed. Even though I was not there, I heard the stories and eventually witnessed part of the outcome. Stealing is a disgusting thing, but trashing a cabin for the thrill of it is a nauseating act of stupidity.

As a general rule, we did not leave alcohol in the cabin: it invited disaster. The first break-in occurred over the winter when the cabin was closed up and unused. Because it is located on an island in the middle of the lake, access occurs only by boat or float plane. In the winter, though, anyone can get to the island over the ice. Virtually everyone in the area has a snow machine, and most likely the first break in was a group of people who decided to have a party with little chance of getting caught during the winter when activity was minimal on the lakes.

Many cabin owners in Alaska do not lock their doors. Locked doors invite door damage, and if someone wants access to a cabin either out of desperation or for malicious purposes, a good stiff kick is all that is usually required. If the door is locked, the jamb is splintered, and repairs can be costly. The debate whether a locked door will really keep out intruders is moot...if someone wants in bad enough it will happen. Nonetheless, as a society we tend to lock our doors, regardless.

The back door to the cabin was, indeed, kicked in, and the intruders found a supply of stashed alcohol and/or brought their own. Stored food was used to cook a big meal and a fire was started in the little-used wood stove to heat the place. These deeds by themselves are not so bad, but because there was little firewood available, the revelers broke up furniture and burned it in the stove. The cooking was messy, the cleanup nonexistent. In fact, it appeared they took every effort to make a mess. Dried food, sauce, and spilled ingredients were everywhere. But the good news is that the cabin was intact. Nothing was damaged that couldn't be fixed by elbow grease, repairs, and money.

Subsequent break-ins took a more malicious toll. At one time, intruders defecated and urinated on bedding, but otherwise the physical damage to the cabin was minimal. After the first break-in, a few preventative measures took place. The "garage," so named only because it had a garage door, was made impervious to assault. Built out of the same stout timbers as the cabin but without windows, the only access was through the single garage door. After the break-in, that door was beefed up with another layer of plywood. The springs that aided in the opening of the door were no match for the added weight/mass of the new door, and therefore, it took two men and a boy to open it. Over time, we rigged a temporary pulley mechanism to open the door while we were there so a single human being of average size and strength could do the deed alone without developing a hernia in the process. Anything valuable or intoxicating was stored in the garage, but outside of a Texas chainsaw intruder, no one was breaking into that fortress.

The second time that the Kellys joined us, the plan was for both planeloads to arrive at the same time. However, that year we all decided to go early in June in order to get to the rainbows before they camouflaged themselves in the thick runs of salmon. Jamo had checked with locals regarding the lake conditions, and while the ice was not completely out, the lake would be open enough for the planes to land, or so we were told. When we arrived we discovered that most of the lake was ice free but not anywhere near where we had to land. Winds had shifted the lake ice and the island was completely surrounded by hard water. After a flyover, a hasty decision was made to fly back to the Agulapak and camp out there at the cabin used by the state park volunteers. It was early enough in the season that no one else was using the cabin, and we hoped our stay would only be a short one until the ice shifted away from the island so we could access our normal accommodations.

The Agulapak cabin is primitive. I'm not sure when it was built, but it was an old frame structure with no insulation or amenities except for the million dollar view from its perch above the river. More importantly, the tin roof did not leak and so we could at least stay dry. As previously mentioned, each year it is occupied for most of the summer by state park volunteers, typically young college students from out of state who donate their time in return for an Alaskan adventure. They are almost always fresh faced and naïve, but learn quickly about bears and mosquitoes in Alaska. We had been inside the cabin briefly on several occasions, usually to fill out a questionnaire about the quality of our experience.

Once we realized that we could not get to the cabin on Aleknagik, we turned around and flew over to Lake Beverly after notifying the Kellys on the plane's radio. We landed and tied the planes on the beach a couple of hundred yards from the cabin situated on a low bluff above the river. The Agulapak is a short river but large in terms of water volume. The wide mouth funnels into a swift current with a multitude of rapids. Sailing down the river in a float-plane would be no fun, so we gave the mouth due respect and parked a safe distance away from the current. Our flyover had pretty much guaranteed the cabin would be empty and it was. With no occupants it was even more primitive than I had remembered: make-shift plywood counters in the "kitchen" would suffice, but beds were in sorry shape—old broken army cots with stained plywood for mattresses greeted us—and as a result, several of us slept on the floor on lumpy life jackets instead.

Groceries were not a problem: we had lots of food. Unfortunately, we only had a one-burner backpacking stove for cooking...a challenge for feeding five hungry men. Nonetheless we made the best of a bad situation and with a minimum of pans, utensils, and cooking supplies, we managed to survive for a couple of days until the ice finally shifted on the lake. Jamo became the head chef; he creatively cooked meals for all of us on the single burner stove—no small feat.

Taking temporary shelter on the Agulapak

After a day or two of suffering this way, Jamo returned from a reconnaissance run with semi-good news: the ice was still packed in front of the cabin, but we could land on the back side of the island and hoof it over the hill to the cabin—which we did. We packed up all our gear into the planes, flew the short distance to Aleknagik, and landed safely on the western side of the island. The cabin was a sight for sore eyes when we came over the ridge, but upon closer inspection, we realized that it had once again been broken into and was a mess. This time the damage was mostly superficial, and despite being disheartened with the discovery, we set about cleaning it up and moving in. The intruders had successfully left the place in shambles, and even though we eventually got the place looking normal, it is a sorry statement that people will go to such lengths to create misery for others.

Generally speaking, the rule of the land is to expect anyone using a cabin to leave it the way they found it. Unoccupied cabins have saved many people in the remote wilderness. A place to dry out, get warm, and find some basic sustenance can be the difference between life and death, so trashing a place seems incredibly senseless. In the old days, the penalties for acts of this kind were justifiably severe.

17

Asleep at the Wheel

Our transportation to the holy fishing grounds was the Parrishes' Cessna 185. They bought the plane new and three of the brothers learned to fly. It was a beautiful plane and well equipped with the latest instrumentation. I'm no aviation expert by any stretch, but most pilots are detail oriented since their lives depend on it. The plane had a STOL kit that made it relatively impervious to stalling, and the plane in general was well maintained. It was equipped with huge PK floats that, while heavy and not particularly aerodynamic, had the benefit of large compartments capable of carrying all sorts of gear, which they did.

Originally we were constantly admonished about where to step, what not to do, and so forth, and over time these things became part of the rituals that needed no further explanation. When things go wrong with an airplane, convenient places to land may or may not be available: we respected the equipment no matter how trivial the precautions might be. Either Jack or I would pump the floats while the plane was being loaded, and Jamo, as pilot, scrutinized the prop, engine, etc. Rarely did any major issue occur—most likely due to the preventative maintenance. However, we did have a couple of mishaps involving the plane and even though I hate to give away an exciting ending, we lived to tell about it.

Occasionally we would be at the cabin late enough in the summer to catch the beginning of the silver salmon run which generally occurred later in July and early August. While we did not often deliberately fish for salmon, silvers (also called cohos) were an exception. Like rainbows, they are great fun to catch, can put on spectacular acrobatic feats, and since they are spawning and on a death march, we would keep them to eat from time to time. In fact, on several occasions we saved the last day or two of the trip exclusively for silvers so we could bring fresh salmon back to Fairbanks.

Typically, we would fish for them in a stretch of the Nushagak River called the "cut bank." The Nushagak at this locale is a big, semi-muddy river, not to mention a main artery for spawning salmon and other species. The "cut bank" was a decent spot to land, had shallow stretches for wading, and the fishing was generally good—even with flies. It was also a fairly short flight from the cabin although close enough to the ocean to be influenced by the tides, so rising or falling tides were a consideration when tying up the plane as well as determining when the fishing would be good. On this one trip and after consulting the tide books, we knew the tide would be going out and the only place to tie the plane was the top of the high bank where we found some brush. Jack scrambled up the 20-foot bank with the rope, and we tied the plane off by the stinger, nose pointing out into the river as was our custom.

The heavy floats needed to be just that, floating, and because the river was dropping with the tide, we knew we would have to monitor the river level and slide the plane further into the river periodically to keep it from becoming high and dry. After fishing for a while by the plane, the three of us spread out along the shore and Jamo and I eventually decided to walk around the bend downstream from the plane. Jack decided to stay there and fish.

"Watch the plane, Jack, and make sure to move it if necessary," Jamo advised.

"No problem...I'll be right here," Jack replied. I'll take care of it."

As long as it was floating, it was a simple matter to let some rope out and slide it further into the river, even single handedly.

Jamo and I headed downstream as planned, and after about an hour of slow fishing with little luck, we decided to head back and see if Jack was catching anything. Chatting amiably as we rounded the bend, we both suddenly stopped dead in our tracks.

There sat Jack comfortably sprawled on the front of the float and leaning back against the strut—chin on his chest, sound asleep. And there sat the plane—beached high and dry. Tiny wavelets daintily splashed against the front of the pontoons. The rest of the plane sat on sand and gravel.

Profanity ensued. Planes are not exactly lighter than air—this one probably weighed over 3000 pounds empty—and moving the floats alone without a Cessna 185 fuselage and engine squatting on top of them would have been a task, but with water barely lapping the front of the floats as the plane sat facing the river, we knew we were screwed. Jack's sleeping, like Rip Van Winkle's, is the stuff of legends, but this was a serious situation.

We awoke Jack, dazed and confused, and he seemed just as surprised as we were to see the pontoons under him completely out of the water. His embarrassment was palpable, but we had work to do. Criticism had to wait.

We untied the plane and the three of us tried to budge it—to no avail. It might as well have been in cement. We could slightly rock it on its floats but could gain not an inch toward the river. Our tide book had previously disclosed this to be an extreme high tide, and the river would not be coming back anywhere near that level, at least in the foreseeable future, so we knew we had to do whatever it took to move the plane, heavy as it was, immediately. The situation would only get worse with time. Jamo climbed in, started the engine, and Jack and I grabbed the push handles on each side of the tail section near the stinger, our feet braced for duty.

Standing directly behind a plane at even partial throttle is noisy and windy, but a 185 at full throttle on a rocky beach is inherently dangerous. My hat and sunglasses immediately sailed off my head as rocks and sand pummeled us, but we kept pushing. At first, nothing happened, but then after a bit it began to budge—ever so slightly. An inch became two, then a foot, then a yard, and with the combined effort of 280 or so horses and Jack and me pushing with everything we had, it finally slid into the water and floated again.

Of course Jack eventually received a due ration of grief for days, if not years, about this. It must be said that we probably did not realize the full extent of the tidal influence initially, and even if we did, it was not a regular event for which we prepared, but really, staying awake being the only prerequisite, any derision he received was deserved. And while that particular lesson did not repeat itself, we still had other lessons to learn. Our travails with transportation were not finished.

18

Boy Scout Knots

A favorite river of ours for fishing, the Grant, is usually explored early in the trip. It is a relatively small stream, larger than Lynx Creek by far but often no more than knee or thigh deep and home to some nice local rainbows. For the most part it requires a degree of stealth, a favorite subject of Jamo's lectures. It is only fair that walking up the river we trade off the lead position which determines who gets first shot at the fish. We have to walk up the middle of the river since the banks are basically impenetrable with thick brush, waist high ferns, and deadfall, and as a result, we spread out to let the fish settle down after someone has passed through a section of the river. We fish this river often, and since certain spots tend to bear the best results, careful strategy requires leaping ahead at just the right places to get the best chance to hook a nice rainbow. This strategy begins soon after we arrive, so it can be a bit of a race to get a fly rod rigged and nonchalantly begin flogging the water ahead of the others while acting as unhurried as possible.

After arriving at our traditional parking spot on the lake, we grab our rods and the posturing begins. We spread out and slowly make our way up the river. If a hole is productive, it makes sense to stay and drain it of all fish for those stumbling behind, especially if they are out of sight, but if none are biting, then moving on keeps you in the lead slot...at least that is the theory. Fishing etiquette dictates giving up the lead once you land a nice fish—although I suspect the rules are sometimes played loosely. As we progress up the river, the distance separating us grows until we are out of sight of one another but still only minutes apart. A short ways from the mouth some legendary holes exist that nearly always produce nice fish and getting there first can create a bit of a race, although no one is actually running. We each carefully stroll up the stream, drifting flies down both sides, especially over and around rocks and logs, but getting to the next prime hole first is always the unspoken goal.

The river is a classic. Jagged deadfall, delicate, bright green fiddlehead ferns, and thick alder and willow line the banks along with thick stands of Spruce and Cottonwood. Periodic streams and rivulets run over mossy cut banks into eddies forming on the sides. Algae covered rocks and boulders conceal the river bottom, and changing currents and run-off bubble over gravel riffles and through occasional deep holes. Looking south and west toward the lake, lofty snowcapped peaks interrupt the skyline. This is truly God's country...not to mention bear country.

But on this one foray up the river, we mutually agreed to forego the preliminaries and hike directly to a spot where lunkers were likely, a gravel bar on a narrow strip maybe a mile or so upstream where big rainbows tend to lurk under brush and timber. Jamo probably thinks of it as his hole since he was first to discover it many odd years ago on our first trip to the spot. The entire length of the river, which we've hiked several times, is probably only five miles or so, but it is a grunt walking upstream against a swift knee deep current most of the way and made even trickier negotiating slime covered rocks in the deeper passages. Regardless, on this day we force-marched our way upriver without tossing a fly in the water except for occasional holes where temptation proved too strong.

We all eventually arrived at the gravel bar a little short of breath from the endeavor, and after fishing for a while, sat and pulled a snack out of our backpacks. It was a good spot for a break, especially after the march to get there.

"Did you tie up the plane, Larry?" Jamo asked as a matter of record and routine. He never tied the plane; Jack or I always did and always with the same proven knots as required by Jamo, essentially a slip knot so that we could untie the plane as easily as we tied it. The rope went through the stinger of the plane and was pulled taut through another slip knot loop in the main line before securing it with a final slip knot. It was simple and efficient.

"Nope. Jack did," I replied.

"I didn't tie up the plane! I thought you did," Jack added, his voice raised for emphasis.

I furrowed my brow and created a picture of the plane sitting in our parking spot. "Are you sure you didn't tie the plane? Because I KNOW I didn't!" I threw back. I mentally retraced my steps. I distinctly remembered putting my rod together and making sure I had everything for the hike upriver. Tying the plane did not conjure up any images.

Our parking spot was a bitch to taxi to as the lake was filled with large boulders that we had to negotiate just below the surface, but once there the brush for tying the stinger off was only a few feet away. We'd been there many times before, and always tied up in the same spot. Despite the difficulty in getting there, the tie up was easy.

We all looked at each other in disbelief. Here we were about 1-1/2 miles up the river, and it was becoming readily apparent it could be the proverbial creek without the paddle...or more accurately...without the plane. After a bit more deliberation, it became clear...no one tied the fucking plane. After parking, each of us had been so rushed to start flogging for fish that no one took responsibility for the tie up. The plane was just sitting on the edge of the lake...we hoped.

Immediately we began a return forced march downstream. Walking down this river is considerably easier than walking upstream against the current, but the moss-covered rocks are no less slippery. Little discussion occurred, or even fishing for that matter—although I'm pretty sure Jack couldn't resist casting through a few holes as we marched by them. He truly is a pig when it comes to fishing.

We set a record time for the distance covered. As we came down the final stretch of river, I secretly prayed nothing had happened to our transportation. We were a long ways from any other sign of life.

We arrived at the mouth of the creek, hurrying but not quite running, and looked longingly around the corner at our parking spot.

The plane...drumroll...the plane...was by the grace of God still there, and as was later revealed, we had not, in fact, tied it to the shore. It was just sitting there bobbing gently in the water. Any breeze could have carried it off into the middle of the lake like an unfurled sailboat. We were probably all to blame, but especially Jack and I since we were in such a hurry to start fishing that we neglected to take care of business first. And because Jamo never tied the plane unless he was by himself...the responsibility lay with us. It was a lesson we never forgot. For many days thereafter, Jack and I verbally checked with each other that the plane was appropriately tied before we left it. Another bullet dodged.

19

Water Runs Downhill

Most of our successful fishing took place in small to moderately sized rivers, but two large systems flow through the heart of the area: the Nushagak and the Nuyakuk. In order to get to the myriad lakes and streams of the area, millions of fish travel these arteries every year. Those fish that enter the Tikchik lake system travel a short ways up the Nushagak delta and then enter the Wood River, which feeds them into Lake Aleknagik. From there they can travel through the connecting rivers to Lake Nerka, Beverly, and Kulik, not to mention a number of smaller lakes, many with no name.

The Nushagak River starts in the drainages about 100 or so miles north of the cabin and migrates in a southeasterly meander until the Nuyakuk flows into it just above the village of Kaliganek where it nearly doubles in size. Shortly after that it gradually turns southwest and eventually enters Bristol Bay at Dillingham where it forms a broad delta. Both of these rivers are major migratory routes for a variety of salmon species, and the guided fishermen are often lured to the area by these fish. Salmon are hefty, great eating, and fun to catch. But we are after the rainbows. Nonetheless, because rainbows thrive on salmon eggs, find the salmon and you'll invariably find trout.

Over the years we tended to wear out the tried and true fishing holes, but we also ventured forth into new territory in search of adventure and, more importantly, big 'bows. Big river fishing is not particularly attractive for several reasons: it is sometimes difficult to fish from shore, it is harder to "see" the fish, but more to the point, we initially had only fair to middling luck most of the time. We learned over the years that, depending on water level, access to gravel bars and riffles could translate into big rainbows on these rivers. Our luck improved when we started motoring up the rivers in the inflatable and then drifted back, one person rowing and two fishing. Once a fish was hooked, we bailed out of the boat and worked the riffle, bank, etc. until we could catch no more fish. The upper Nushagak proved especially fruitful for this technique, and since the river was big, we always had plenty of room to stretch out and not step on one another, even if other people like the Kellys were with us.

As we aged and our trips took place in the new millennium, we grew adventuresome and branched out into areas on the map not scrutinized previously. This usually resulted in flyovers looking for likely spots: eddies, riffles, gravel bars, etc. and then finding a suitable landing spot downstream so we would always motor upstream. That way, if bad things happened to the motor, we could always float and row back to the plane.

One such excursion took us to the lower Nuyukuk just above where it meets the Nushagak. As you might expect, the confluence was a big-water area, and Jamo landed upstream on the slightly smaller Nuyukuk rather than fight the current of the Nushagak.

The Nuyukuk, however, is nothing to sneeze at for river speed and volume. It drains Tikchik Lake in a glorious series of falls, the water cascading thunderously into deep pools and over huge boulders. On previous trips we had landed above and below the falls and viewed them from either side. The sheer volume of water hurtling over the precipices never failed to impress us from the air, but standing next to them was breathtaking—and loud.

Fishing can be great along the river's length, but we had never tried down near the confluence with the Nushagak so we tied off, pumped up the boat, and headed upstream. However, the fishing proved to be of no great consequence, so we decided to head down to the confluence and up the Nushagak where further upstream we had spotted some promising channels. This meant we had to head downstream below the plane for a short ways or else deflate the boat, load everything back into the plane, take off, and land again. We decided to leave the plane where it sat since we were already fully geared for fishing in the boat.

Flying over a river at 100 knots is deceiving—long distances appear shorter under those conditions. The areas that had looked promising from the plane took a bit longer to get to, but in the end paid out. We had some incredible fishing where all three of us landed numerous nice sized rainbows. We continued upstream and the fishing stayed consistently good for much of the day. Eventually, though, we realized it was getting late, and reluctantly we started working our way back to the plane, the late evening setting sun blinding us as we came down the river. The swift current aided our speed.

Always on the lookout for more fish, Jack noticed a channel we had missed on the way up, and he motioned for Jamo to pull into it. We pulled the boat up onto a gravel bar and worked the bank to no avail for 20 minutes or so. Finally, we agreed we had had enough, it was getting late, and whiskey loomed large back at the cabin. We packed up our rods, pushed off, and Jamo pulled the starter rope of the 15-horse Johnson. Nothing happened. The rope wouldn't unwind. Then he realized the throttle was in gear instead of neutral, locking the starter. The problem was...it wouldn't go into neutral. It was stuck in gear.

"What the fuck is this all about?" he said to no one in particular. He pulled the cowling off the engine and worked the gearshift. Shift, it did not. By now Jack had taken an interest. My attention was just getting aroused.

"You realize, of course, that the plane is UPSTREAM on the Nuyukuk?" I proffered. This was not exactly a startling revelation, but stressing the importance of the motor seemed a good thing to do. I was mentally picturing the confluence—a swift corner, big and wide, with probably a 4 plus mile current to overcome. I looked at the diminutive paddles affixed to the raft. Jack regularly broke them just rowing across quiet sections of river. How would they hold up to this?

My observation did not go unnoticed. Both Jack and Jamo realized that if we didn't get the motor working, we were screwed. We could always drift to Kaliganek and hope someone would run us up to the plane, but that was a plan way on down the alphabet of options at this point.

Meanwhile, Jamo had figured out what was wrong, but the issue of actually fixing it lay unresolved. A critical piece of linkage had come undone, and without it, the motor would not go into neutral—hence—the motor could not be started and would not run. We had tools. We had electrical tape. We had an engineer, a lawyer, and a teacher. All we needed was a candlestick maker. Nothing was working though.

Eventually deft fingers and needle nosed pliers were able to snake the parts back together, and with a piece of wire from some other spare part, we could get the motor in neutral and back into gear. We breathed a sigh of relief. Success was ours—along with a stern reminder about the inviolate rule of never traveling below the plane, even briefly.

All the way down the river Jamo wore the cowling like a welding helmet, afraid to put it back on the engine and jinx our progress. In short order we came to the confluence and successfully navigated our way upstream to the plane. Each of us realized, as well, that there was no chance we could have rowed back to the plane. Once again we had cheated Fate.

Captain Jamo and his racing "helmet"

20

Piloting Perils

On numerous occasions we did have to camp out due to bad weather. This happened occasionally on the flights to and from Fairbanks, but more often when we were returning to the cabin from fishing in the area. Jack and I tended to be somewhat cavalier about clouds, but Jamo was much more circumspect, and in the end, we always respected the wisdom of the pilot.

"There are old pilots and there are bold pilots, but there are few old, bold pilots," Jamo would each time remind us.

Minor discomfort camping in the rain was balanced by the realization that we were alive. Flying in SW Alaska is deceiving, and many examples exist of pilots and passengers who paid for their mistakes with their lives. It seems that every year a plane flies into a mountain somewhere in Alaska, and often in the regions we frequent. The terrain typically looks flat, but in reality it rises gradually in many places so that what seems like an easy passage over level ground gradually and deceivingly puts the plane in the clouds. The danger is, of course, that invisible hills and mountains can then get in the way. Finding mountains in the clouds while flying tends to be unforgiving and it happens to bold pilots regularly.

Because of this, emergency provisions were always first to go into the plane. These included basic food items: freeze dried meals and perhaps a can of chili or something easily heated, dry clothes since we were always dressed in fishing gear (either neoprene or Gore-Tex waders), sleeping bags, and a dose of whiskey...originally either Jamo's or Jack's but eventually both. The whiskey was never opened unless and until we absolutely knew we were spending the night. If we thought we might be able to simply wait out a squall, we did just that and the booze lay untouched. When, in fact, we came to the conclusion that camping was in the cards, we got on with it, gathering any dry wood we could find, building a fire, and setting up the tent. As elder boy scouts, we were all adept at setting up camp.

Originally, due to space considerations we carried a single foam sleeping pad and several life jackets for emergency beds. The pad belonged to Jamo, and he always took it while Jack and I slept on the lumpy life jackets. Since Jack could sleep standing up, or in any position for that matter, comfort posed no problem for him. I typically was able to grab minutes rather than hours of sleep on top of my life jacket bed, so it is fair to say I did not look forward to these occasions. Each time we camped out I would uncomfortably lie there listening to my comrades' buzz saw snoring for most of the night. Other than the sleeping arrangements, the accommodations were fine— freeze dried meals did the job and we were always safe and dry no matter the weather. That same old backpacking stove that we used on the Agulapak faithfully provided hot water for many a meal over the years. And since it could operate on avgas, fuel was never in short supply: we simply had to drain it from a wing tank.

Later, toward the end of our plane travels, we had the use of a satellite phone. While this could not change the weather, it allowed us to communicate with aviation weather channels so we could at least have an idea of just how long we might be grounded. The bottom line, though, was typical for Alaskan weather prediction: look up in the sky and what you see is what you get. Cloudy weather is not unusual or necessarily dangerous, but low ceilings created a danger due to the previously described rise and fall of the terrain, not to mention the mountains all around the lakes. The plane's navigational aides provided only moderate help, and Jamo's conservative decisions probably saved our lives regularly.

Originally, we flew without any sophisticated equipment other than a VOR and a map. At some point the Parrishes acquired a Lorraine receiver that showed our position as long as it could triangulate the radio signals sent out over Alaska from giant towers located around the state. The problem was that every time we needed it for navigation, we would get a weak signal that could not be trusted and the bright red letters "WARN" would flash across the instrument's screen. Even if the location indicator seemed correct, we couldn't rely on it.

In time, though, satellite navigation became standard in the plane, and the addition of a global positioning system gave us much more reliable information and flexibility, especially for the long trip to and from the area. But even though a GPS could show us where we were, it could not show us where the mountains were in enough detail to warrant flying in the clouds. We relied always on visual references.

For years, it seemed like every trip from Fairbanks to the area required a lengthy diversion to McGrath, a decent sized (for rural Alaska) community on the Kuskokwim River. We stopped there so often due to poor weather in our early years that it felt like a regular waypoint: we had the menu at the local restaurant memorized. The diversion to McGrath was considerably out of the way, but weather in the area south of there was often marginal or a crap-shoot. The 1000-foot ceiling needed for clearance over the "pass" to sneak into the Nushagak drainage was often iffy. And as reported, finding it is even harder at lower altitude where terrain tends to blend and all look the same. A GPS, however, eventually allowed us to pinpoint the pass even with relatively low ceilings, thereby eliminating the need to stop at McGrath to get a weather report complemented with a cheeseburger.

On one of those early trips, we ran into some cloudy weather, but forged ahead as things didn't seem too bad, at least for the moment—so much so that I was casually reading a book in the back of the plane instead of paying attention to potential dangers. This was one of the early trips when Jack stayed up front, occasionally nodding off but keeping moderately alert. Suddenly, I was distracted from my reading by the screeching buzz of the stall warning screaming in the plane over the already loud noise of the plane's engine— something that never happened. I looked up and sat upright at what I saw.

Everything was white! The horizon, the ground, everything outside the window was gone and replaced by a white sheet. Even depth perception was gone. Add to this the continuous noise of the stall warning, and I was on full alert. Jamo was all business.

"Grab my visor out of the pouch behind my seat," he yelled. I wouldn't describe him as panicked, but his request had an urgency I'd not heard before.

Flying without visual reference is a creepy feeling, to say the least, and you lose all sense of direction including which way is up or down. We were climbing steadily according to the altimeter, pedal to the metal, as it were, and executing a 180-degree turn in hopes we could regain visual reference in the area we had just passed through. Every glance out the window resulted in dizziness. I could only imagine trying to fly the plane under these conditions.

I handed Jamo the visor and he put it on in place of his baseball hat. The visor was actually a "hood" which allowed him only a view of the instrument panel so he wouldn't get disoriented by looking out the windows, and I could see why— my senses were in complete disarray as I peered out the side window looking for any kind of landmark or skyline. For what seemed like an eternity but probably lasted only a few minutes, my heart was in my throat. No one said a word beyond Jamo's initial profanity when he realized we were in the clouds. The engine roared at full throttle and the stall warning unnervingly screamed throughout the event.

We had been flying in the middle of a broad valley a safe distance from any obstacles, but the mountains on either side seemed suddenly to be looming in the impermeable fog surrounding the plane. We continued our vigil silently.

"There—I see the ground," Jack shouted, now clearly alert and wide awake. A small hole in the vast whiteness surrounding the plane appeared below us off the starboard side.

Without a hesitation Jamo redirected the plane to the visible topography and we dove toward the spot as if we were on the tail of Baron Von Richthofen. We broke through the hole in the clouds and regained our visual reference with earth, all breathing a sigh of relief. The ground had never looked so good.

Most passengers in commercial planes think nothing of flying in the clouds and I've become so cavalier, I rarely look out the window anymore in a jetliner—it is an everyday occurrence to fly on instruments in commercial airliners that fly ABOVE the mountains. However, it is not something that Jamo had any desire to do, and even though he did have an instrument rating, visibility with the ground was the best instrument we had. Once we could see terra firma after our brief but intense scare, we plotted a different route and swung out of our way for another unscheduled stop in McGrath to check weather. After landing and getting a cheeseburger at our favorite restaurant, we took off from the river and made it to the cabin safely that evening.

The flight is long—nearly five hours—in fairly cramped quarters, and we typically stop on some unnamed lake somewhere in the middle of nowhere to pee. It is usually no big deal: we land, get on the float, and do our business. It is way better than trying to pee in a bottle while flying, the other alternative. I learned early on about excess liquid intake before departure and the benefit of peeing anytime the opportunity presented itself. The constant vibration of the plane only increased bladder production.

"Anyone have to pee?" The question always elicited affirmative responses. Jamo would check the wind direction based on the waves on the lake, and set the plane down somewhere in the middle. He would shut down the engine and enjoying the momentary quiet, we would unfasten our seatbelts, shoulder harnesses, and headsets and scramble out onto the float, me on the passenger side if I was the co-pilot and Jack and Jamo on the left side. Getting out of the back is a bit of a struggle. Jamo would get out from his pilot's seat and reach in and grab the lever to slide the seat forward. The back seat passenger would then climb out, carefully stepping on the strut before landing on the float.

We were all out of the plane, the waves lapping gently against the pontoons and the steady flow of urine hitting the lake the only sounds available.

"Oh shit," Jack screamed—briefly followed by a loud splash. Jack fell in...not quite completely before Jamo was able to grab him—with his free hand, and pull him back onto the float.

"Jesus, we haven't even got there and you are already wet!" Jack had a penchant for falling in the rivers in his efforts to get to places no one else could reach. Of course one person's misfortune is another's glee: we got a fair amount of mileage out of the episode at Jack's expense. Watching someone fall in water never fails to amuse and Jack was an expert. Soaking wet, he piled into the back of the plane for the remainder of the flight.

As many times as we made the flight to and from the region, we never took it for granted. It is easy to become lackadaisical with routines, and a nearly five-hour flight lends itself to false assumptions about safety and security. I always felt more at ease if we were cruising at 3000 feet or so, but Jamo liked to fly at lower altitudes, mainly because you can see much more detail closer to the ground. We were always on the lookout for game, and the changing topography is much more interesting at lower altitudes. The glide path from 800 feet to the ground is much shorter, though, especially if we were to have an engine failure...a point I never forgot.

Jamo would invariably ask whoever was in the co-pilot's seat to take over from time to time. Flying a plane once it is airborne is not all that difficult. It is different than driving a car, however. Wind is always a factor and staying on course can be tricky, especially with only minimal navigational aides.

Since I was usually the co-pilot to and from Fairbanks, I got in my share of flying time. Keeping the plane on course became my focus since Jamo would use any wanderings off course as a chance to unload criticism on whoever was flying the plane. Before we had the Lorraine or the GPS, we documented our route by cross checking the visual references out the window with the map. For the uninitiated, this can be tricky. Cross checking a two-dimensional map with three-dimensional visual references was often a challenge. Usually it required figuring out the elevation of the surrounding hills and mountains and finding those landmarks on the map in front of you. And because the course necessitated changes in direction at various waypoints, knowing where you were was essential to not ending up in the wrong part of the country and surrounded by tall mountains.

When the Lorraine and later the GPS were added to the plane, the route was electronically displayed on the screen so that keeping on the correct path was much easier. Jamo would usually take a brief nap if he felt things were going well, and either Jack or I were left to our own devices controlling the plane. Jack often had a tendency to fly the plane with the starboard wing dipping lower than the port side. This prompted Jamo as critic and instructor to give him an Asian pseudonym, Won Wing Lo.

On those long flights to and from home, Jamo would often test me. On one flight I wore the hood for about 45 minutes flying at low levels through valleys while he monitored our progress visually. With the hood on, I could only see the instrument panel, my eyes on the altimeter to ensure we were not gaining or losing altitude and the bubble indicator to keep the wings level. The GPS showed any variation from the established route mapped out in advance, and Jamo would fine-tune it so that a variation of ¼ mile looked like we had veered completely off route by several miles. This made flying not only challenging, but also interesting.

Flying the plane was the only way to keep Jack awake in it. Otherwise, he would last only a few minutes and be sound asleep, completely unaware how close we were to death at any given moment. Once we got near the fishing, though, he would wake up in anticipation of slaying some rainbows.

Jack also flew longer sections of the flight from time to time as well, and on one return trip, he sat in the copilot's seat while I read in the back. Jamo handed over the controls and after giving Jack basic instructions, closed his eyes for a nap. I continued with my novel, oblivious to our progress.

After about 30 minutes, Jamo woke up and looked around. He grabbed the map and studied it for a few minutes, occasionally looking out the window with a perplexed frown. Finally he looked over at Jack.

"Where the fuck are we, Jack?"

Jack, hands firmly on the yoke, replied defensively, "We're on course...where do you think we are?"

"I think we are about 50 miles off the route and in restricted air space!" Jamo's tone had sharpened. He pointed to the GPS and then to the map. "Jesus, we're headed to Denali Park!" You need to reset your course.

I looked up from the back, mildly concerned but mainly laughing inside at Jack's consternation and embarrassment. I also knew how easy it was to get off course, so I was glad he was on the receiving end of the remarks and not me. Jamo's criticisms of our piloting skills kept us aware that bad things can happen in a hurry in a small plane, and in the final analysis, it was all about staying alive for another future trip.

One other bit of plane excitement occurred during one of the two times General Jim was staying with us. The General was a helicopter pilot, and had thousands of hours in Viet Nam as well as domestically. Jamo clearly respected his skills as a pilot, and even though he spent much less time in fixed wing aircraft, he was a veteran of flying a variety of planes.

The weather had been foul, and we were landlocked for several days. Wind and rain howled outside the cabin, but more importantly we couldn't see the mountain on the opposite shore of the lake, our barometer for flying weather. If we couldn't view the mountain across the lake, the chances were slim that we would have enough visibility to the north of us where most of the fishing occurred. Even though we couldn't actually see in that direction from the cove where the cabin sat, the view across the lake was a dependable weather report. Also, if flying was even marginal, we would hear the guides flying over the cabin. The airways, though, were silent.

General Jim spent long periods of time staring out the large windows looking across the lake and wishing the clouds and fog away. He was only with us for a limited period, and every day cabin bound was one less day he could fish.

All of us were getting cabin fever, and finally Jamo raised our hopes, "I think it is lifting. I can see about half way up the hillside now." We all got up from our books and looked out the window. It did look slightly brighter, but the wind continued to howl and the lake had white caps rolling in a NW direction toward the cabin.

Finally, after another 30 minutes, we could see most of the mountain across the lake.

"I don't think it is good enough to fly over the saddle, but we could go to the end of the lake and check out the Agulowok." Jamo's observation perked us up. The Agulowok flowed from Lake Nerka to the north of us into Lake Aleknagik. It was a short river—only a mile or two long, but it ran swift and deep. We had never fished much beyond the mouth where it entered Aleknagik—it was too big to walk up and steep banks defined either side. Also, because the guides in nearby lodges fished it regularly, we avoided it. However, at least we would be getting out of the cabin and getting our lines in the water.

We grabbed our fishing gear and changed into waders and rain jackets. It was by any definition a nasty day but we dressed appropriately. Jamo readied the plane and set up a couple of temporary seats in the back. Since there were four of us, the General with his flying experience would sit up front with Jamo, and Jack and I would take up the back. We pumped the accumulated water out of the floats, threw our gear into the plane, and loaded up.

Getting in the back of a 185 takes a bit of dexterity. It is a tight space even when it is not loaded with tackle boxes, fly rods, and other paraphernalia. Jack and I slid the front seats all the way forward and squeezed in, each sitting on a make shift perch with the lap belts our only security in case of a hard landing. Jamo and General Jim piled in, and after the preliminaries, Jamo fired up the big engine.

It became readily apparent that this would not be an ordinary take off. Unlike cars, small planes do not have windshield wipers and the visibility out front was a blur at best. Wind generated by the plane's airspeed is the only thing that cleans the water off the windshield and taxiing in a heavy rainstorm was not cutting it.

Jamo and Jim both opened the side windows and the wind from the prop filled the cabin. The plane rocked up and down on the floats as we taxied through the large whitecaps, getting bigger the further we traveled from shore. After checking the instruments and warming the engine, we slowly circled looking skyward for any traffic. No surprise, we were the only ones foolish enough to be flying.

"All set?" Jamo asked. We gave him the thumbs up and he closed his window, latched it, and pushed the throttle to the firewall.

With four of us, we were not a light load, but the plane began racing toward the opposite shore with deliberate acceleration bouncing through the rough water. The wind direction forced us to take off across lake on the short path to the opposite shore. I grabbed the handhold above the window in a white knuckled grip, and eventually we were skimming on top of the waves. The wind was blowing hard enough that our air speed quickly jumped up and Jamo pulled back on the yoke to pop the floats off the water. The plane responded accordingly and we jumped into the air. Jamo adjusted the flaps one notch at a time and our airspeed increased. Because of the short distance to the other side of the lake, he immediately banked the plane to the west, and that's when the fun began.

Even in the short time we were loading the plane, we were soaked from the rain. When Jamo banked the plane, the wind coming from the southeast became a tail wind and the plane shot down the lake in a westerly direction. At the same time, all the windows immediately fogged up from all the moisture in the cabin, and we couldn't see a thing.

"Shit," was all Jamo said. "Quick, hand me some paper towel." We always kept a roll in the plane for various purposes. Jack ripped off a wad and handed it up front. As fast as Jamo wiped the windshield, it quickly fogged over again. Finally he opened his side window and the combination of freezing wind and constant wiping cleared the windshield enough so we could see.

My grip on the handhold above me never loosened until we landed.

The lake is about 10 miles long so the trip to the Agulowok was a short one. By the time we got there, we could see out all the windows again, and Jamo landed the plane after banking and descending into the wind. The waves continued to rock us as we turned and taxied to the shore by the river mouth.

I think we were all appreciative when we stepped out onto the beach even though the flight only lasted a few minutes. We unloaded our gear, and soon forgot about any potential perils as the first dollies started gulping down flies. The fishing was better than expected and we were soon whooping and hollering, "Fish on."

We all caught a number of nice sized fish, and it provided welcome relief from the cabin fever we had been experiencing while we waited for the weather to lift.

The rain and wind continued off and on throughout the afternoon, and despite the good fishing, eventually we decided to give up and head back to the cabin for drinks and dinner. By then the clouds had given way to occasional swatches of blue sky, and even though we still had to plow through whitecaps as we taxied into the lake, I was somewhat reassured by the fact that the windows did not immediately fog up.

Thankfully, the short flight home was uneventful. Boring can be good, especially in a small airplane.

21

Sartorial Statements

Because Jack fished in a rubber wet suit in our early days, he was never too concerned about staying dry as long as he was warm. Jack is tough: he rarely utters anything resembling a complaint, so when he would go in the drink, which happened with regularity, it was simply shrugged off as an occupational hazard. It also allowed him to take risks that neither Jamo nor I would typically consider. For instance, the Agulapak is maybe three hundred yards wide at the mouth with fast current, slimy boulders, and numerous drop offs and riffles. On more that one occasion, Jack walked all the way across the river to get to better fishing. This is a major feat, especially where Lake Beverly forms the river's headwaters and the current is especially strong.

Walking in the river required a wide stance and a shuffling movement so your feet never really left the bottom. The slippery surface combined with the swift current had a tendency to force a path downstream, which by itself is not too bad but made the return trip against the current all the more exciting. If you happened to get up to your waist in the water, buoyancy also became a factor and disaster was only a misstep away. And even if your feet found purchase on gravel and not a slimy boulder, you could feel them sinking as the current stripped away the sand around your boots, much like the retreating surf will do on an ocean beach. I was way too lily-livered to attempt walking all the way across, so when Jack would scream, "Fish on," I could only look on in envy. He earned those fish since he invariably fell in the process of getting to them.

Fishing in a wet suit was not exactly the fashionable get up of the lodge fishermen who also frequented the Agulapak. But if it was not in style, Jack did not seem to care. His outfit was practical if you ignore wrinkled flesh at the end of the day. At first, he simply wore regular hiking boots that, once dampened, stayed continually wet throughout the trip like the rubber wet suit. Putting wet boots on your feet first thing every day does not sound appealing, and eventually he adopted regular wading boots that, while still keeping his feet wet, at least provided some traction with felt soles. In time, though, he adopted more conventional approaches, and one year, probably in the early 90's, he showed up with a brand new pair of Cabella's neoprene waders. He had retired the wet suit for good.

Jamo always set the trends when it came to gear in our group. He started with neoprene waders and after my first misguided experience with the heavy rubber version, I immediately sent out to Cabella's for some neoprene waders when I knew I would be returning the next year. As an impoverished teacher, not to mention one who at times can be penny-pinching, I decided to make my own wading "boots." Jamo's wading boots looked heavy and cumbersome, but the felt soles provided great traction on the slippery rocks. I had a brainstorm. Felt soles are the same as felt inserts, I reasoned, which are readily available and inexpensive. I purchased a pair and affixed them using massive amounts of Shoo Goo to the bottoms of a pair of bright red Chinese Converse All Star knock-off basketball shoes. I should have realized that even if the colorblind fish didn't see me coming, they would flee in embarrassment from my penurious homemade footgear.

"What the hell are those?" Jamo as loadmaster was placing the gear in the plane as we handed it to him.

"My wading boots," I replied as if anyone could see these would be the newest hip addition to piscatorial fashion.

"You might want a back-up. These don't look too sturdy."

I hadn't really considered bringing a backup. We were so discouraged about bringing required equipment due to weight restrictions that I never considered that weight saved by my "boots" could be used elsewhere.

"Not necessary. You'll see." My bravado was only a shell.

Of course history records that the first time I stepped in a stream for more than 30 seconds, the felt soles attached with a product applied so thickly that King Kong could not pull them apart, or so I thought, immediately started flapping at the toe like the tongue on the cover of the Rolling Stones "Sticky Fingers" album. Immediately, walking became a hazard. I eventually ripped off the felts and spent the remainder of the trip precariously prancing with only the cheap Chinese rubber soles for solace. The next year I had brand new Cabellas' wading boots.

Neoprene waders are warm and dry, so long as they are hole free. Walking in brush and casting large wet flies occasionally resulted in rips and tears, which of course leaked. The fix of choice was Shoo Goo, but as good as it was, once torn, the waders would eventually leak again. It was imperative to avoid the tears in the first place. But by the time Jack and I were firmly settled in to our neoprene waders as the standard for staying dry, Jamo had moved on to Gore-Tex.

Neoprene does have a few drawbacks. Pulling them on is somewhat akin to rubberized panty hose, not that I've tried that, but I have seen my wife go through the motions with the nylon versions. And even though neoprene waders are warm, they are often too much so: they don't breathe. At the end of a long day that invariably involved lots of hiking, I was hot and sticky. On warm days—it can easily be in the 70's where we go—they were unbearable. Further discomfort occurred in the plane where, seated in the back on a make shift seat such as a rubber raft or tackle boxes and combined with the vibration of the aircraft in flight, my buttocks would start itching like a bad rash. Then there was the unpleasant issue of urination and general waste elimination, which required peeling them off and avoid making them a receptacle in the process as they dangled around your feet. Enough said.

So, when Jamo extolled the virtues of Gore-Tex, it sounded great, but my penny-pinching kicked in again and since my neoprene waders were still functional, I couldn't see forking over the funds for new ones. Jamo, who is not a name brand buyer of waders, often buys cheap—namely via Sam's Club or some other discount warehouse. This means that 1) they are probably made inexpensively "overseas," 2) they have limited sizes, and 3) you never know when they will have them back in stock because for sure they'll be out of stock the next time you go there. I did look for Gore-Tex waders, and true to form they only had size XXXL on the shelves, not a good fit for my 5'8" frame. But eventually, my neoprene waders leaked enough that I sucked up my pride and bought an expensive pair of Simms waders, a decision I have never regretted. (I say this without the thought of a possible endorsement check, but I wouldn't turn one down if offered.) Jack also eventually came around as well, so that during the latter years of our adventures together, we all more or less resembled fishermen right out of the catalogs—at least from a distance.

Jamo, again making a cutting edge fashion statement but more for the sake of practicality, was the first to fish with a

126

combo fishing vest/life jacket. When we are in the inflatable, we always wear life jackets and they only add to the bulk from a vest loaded with fly boxes, various tying accouterments, extra leaders, etc. I resembled the Pillsbury Doughboy with my life jacket, but I hated to relinquish the ancient fishing vest given to me as a present by Afton Blanc, a teacher with whom I had worked many years before. It was stained in all the right places and had a tear or two, but it had been a faithful garment for too many years. Nonetheless, I envied the trim look of the combo vest that allowed both Jamo and Jack to eliminate their life jackets since they could now simply inflate their fishing vests while we were cruising up and down the rivers. This had the unintended consequence of eliminating lifejackets for lumpy emergency bedding, but it was a net gain with the addition of real foam sleeping pads for all of us in emergencies.

22

Fishing the Riviera

Over the years we encountered all kinds of weather while fishing, snow being the one exception, thankfully. Coastal weather patterns dominate the region around the lakes, less so the further inland we travelled. The weather at Aleknagik might be rainy and foggy while just north of the Saddle blue skies and warm, even hot (by Alaska standards) temperatures prevailed. And while the streams around the lakes provided much of our fishing mainly due to their proximity, at times we ventured further away, especially when a high pressure system moved in and we had unlimited visibility and great flying.

On those days, we occasionally ventured northwest into the Togiak drainage. The Togiak is a big river with some serious salmon runs, and therefore, it must contain rainbows, or so we figured. The net result, though, was usually disappointing in the fishing department. More accurately, the fishing was great; it was the catching that didn't live up to standards. To get there required flying over the rugged Wood River Range, a formidable series of jagged peaks and a flight we only attempted during spectacular weather. Once the plane climbed over the craggy snow capped mountains, we descended into gorgeous country: mountain lakes and clear streams with grassy banks—classic rainbow rivers. But if the rainbows were in abundance, our track record showed that we were clueless as to how to catch them or get to where they waited for us.

In later years, we tended to explore areas to the north with more positive results—the upper Nushagak River and its feeder streams. The early years of sweaty neoprene waders had given way to much more comfortable Gore-Tex by then, but one summer we experienced several consecutive days of sunny, hot weather. Even breathable Gore-Tex proved too hot. The fact that we rarely left the cabin before noon only served to add to the heat. In fact because the Alaskan days are so long, the evenings remained warm as long as the waning sun peaked over the horizon.

"I'm going for shorts today," Jamo announced as we readied our gear for the day. He appeared in swimming trunks, neoprene socks, and his wading boots. With his snow-white legs, farmer's tan, and clunky wading boots, he reminded me of Jed Clampett at Malibu Beach. Fashion gave way to comfort, however, and soon Jack and I were on board, looking like descendants from the same clan.

The day had started out blazing at the cabin, but the weather could be considerably different a 45 minute flight inland. As a precaution we packed waders and warm gear in a large waterproof Pelican storage box, just in case. We loaded the plane, and soon we were taxiing out of the cove, all three of us comfortable in the heat and looking like we were going to the Riviera, minus the boots, of course. When we arrived on the river, the sun continued to beat down. We inflated the Metzler, loaded our gear, and motored upstream to the fishing.

It was a stunning day—no clouds and temps in the high 70's, but the unknown quantity was the water temperature. The knee-deep eddy water seemed warm enough as we unloaded the plane, but the real test would be standing waist deep in fast-moving current, enduring what I would call the "testicle trial." Our fishing usually required at least moderate wading, but most of our body parts had never really experienced this without the protection of at least Gore-Tex waders. Standing semi-nude for hours in an Alaskan river would be a novel experience for us.

Our first stop at the confluence of the Nushagak and another river resulted in the three of us showing no visible pain as we waded out into the water...it seemed almost bathtub warm once we were in it. Catching rainbow trout dressed in a t-shirt and swimming trunks might be common in the warmer climes of the lower 48, but standing that way in a wild river in Alaska seemed unreal. It worked so well, we eventually got rid of the wading boots and wore only Teva sandals for foot protection. Other than the occasional discomfort of rocks lodging in our sandals, this was the high life. Add great days of fishing to the formula and permanent smiles graced our faces.

I'm not sure if the warm weather or our beautiful legs persuaded the fish, but during those days we seemed to have record rainbow fishing. Standing all day in waist deep water in swimming trunks and sandals while catching big fish eliminated any possible thoughts of discomfort.

This became the modus operandi for many days of fishing. No doubt we received odd stares from guides and clients covered head to toe in Gore-Tex, bug netting, and even rain gear as they occasionally passed by in riverboats. Our exposed skin gave proof as well to the lie that the bugs are always horrible in Alaska. And even though we had warm clothes and waders available if needed, I don't remember ever having to change out once we started with our beach attire. Of course, weather often dictated that beachwear was not an option, and our farmer's tans gave final testimony to more typical fishing fashion.

It doesn't get any better than this!

23

Lewis and Clarke Kent

Over the years, but especially early on in our trips, we did a substantial amount of exploration. Partly, this was due to the desire to conquer new mountains, so to speak, but primarily we did it to find great fishing, especially where we would not run into others with the same idea. While not exactly the Corps of Discovery, we did find ourselves in some untrammeled wilderness after great effort on numerous occasions. The cabin had a huge map of the area on one wall, and it served as our primary research document. Areas that looked promising received a flyover and if we could land and take off from someplace nearby, we pursued them further.

For many of these adventures, especially early on, Jamo would drop off Jack and me, and we would float a river, fishing along the way and meet Jamo at the other end. This selfless act on his part was necessary since neither Jack nor I could fly the plane, so we benefited greatly from our limited skill set. Even if the fishing was not noteworthy, the floating was always enjoyable.

Lake Kulik is connected to Lake Beverly by a relatively short river that is actually divided into two sections—The Wind and The Peace. The river drains Kulik in a hurry, carving a pass through steep rugged mountains, starting with a sharp bend a few hundred yards from the mouth followed by several rapids and a few splits before it forms a lake of sorts in a wide, quiet section. In the raft, the upper section provided brief thrills with its whitewater, one of us paddling while the other fished, occasionally stopping and fishing the banks and rocks of an area that showed promise. The river is decent sized, and while the current cascades swiftly in its channels, the Metzler handled it easily. The scenery and paddling grabbed our attention, but the fishing drew no great exclamations of wonder on that first exploratory trip.

Where the river widens into The Peace sits the stately Golden Horn Lodge. Like most of the lodges in the area, and there are many, the focal point of the resort is a large central lodge with substantial glass for viewing the stunning vistas of the area. Smaller outbuildings, cabins, and a beefy dock for planes and boats also dot the resort. Most of the lodges fly clients to remote areas for fishing, but they also utilize riverboats for more localized use.

Rivers connect the four big lakes, Kulik, Beverly, Nerka, and Aleknagik in series, but travel from Kulik to Aleknagik or even eventually to Dillingham would be a long trip even in a jet boat due to the serpentine nature of the route. So greater distances are usually covered in a floatplane and temporary accommodations are set up for the guides in those remote areas with large platform tents and boats. The blue and yellow Beaver of the Golden Horn Lodge was a familiar site when we were gassing up at Moody's Marina or when it passed overhead as we fished in the area, the stinger rope dangling behind the plane like a banner.

The river below the Golden Horn lodge flows steadily a mile or so to Lake Beverly. It is much wider in this section, which results in a slower drift. We occasionally pulled the boat up and fished, catching a few in the process, but found no magical spots. By the time we got to the lake where Jamo awaited us, he lay stretched out on the bank. He'd fished the mouth, and like us, had mixed results. Regardless, the scenery alone, the stuff of Ansel Adams-like calendars, made the trip worthwhile.

Other floats paid greater dividends—the best occurring in another series of lakes south of Aleknagik, and area we fished less often as a rule. The modus operandi we followed was to land in the lakes and fish the streams and rivers flowing in and out of them. Sometimes we walked or boated up them, but except for the one nearly disastrous occasion on the Nuyakuk, we never boated down them. Getting back to the plane was a priority, and since anything could happen to the boat, we used it to travel only in directions that provided an easy float back to the plane unless Jamo dropped us off.

On this occasion we pumped up the boat and entered a grassy channel that eventually formed a river probably five miles long and ended in a lower lake. Jamo fired up the plane once we were ready to float and we waved goodbye.

The trip began as a slow drift with little current. Immediately, our attentions perked up.

"Bear!" I exclaimed. Jack rowed the inflatable in the traditional fashion, facing the rear as I surveyed the terrain in front of us. Just the mention of that noun caused him to stop rowing and turn quickly around. The channel weaved in a meandering fashion through a grassy swamp defined on one side by a low hill. Lying on the hilltop eating roots or berries was a grizzly bear that appeared average in size from our vantage. Size provides little solace, however, when you are slowly drifting in relatively shallow water easily accessible to a furry critter. The bear seemed to ignore us.

"I don't think he's seen us," I offered in a low voice. Jack was now paying close attention. He had twisted around facing forward, the oars dangling in the water. He carried a stainless

134

steel .44 magnum pistol and now held it in his hand at the ready. The bear was a substantial distance away, probably a couple of hundred yards, but as we drifted slowly down the channel, we realized our wandering path would take us closer to him.

"What do you want to do?" I asked. Unarmed, I at least wanted to explore the contingencies, just in case. The "pucker factor" always rises when a bear is spotted, even if they are a long ways off. We watched him digging and rooting around for several minutes.

Finally he seemed to notice us. He squinted—bears have notoriously bad vision—and nose to the air, sniffed. Once our scent hit him, he stood up on his back legs. Our progress had taken us closer, and any escape route was marginal and probably involved trying to outrun a bear, something not possible. Once he visually located us, his demeanor changed. Bears usually avoid human contact and this, fortunately, was the case. He dropped to all fours and scampered off out of sight over the hill. Nonetheless, he remained in the back of our minds for some time, and we stayed vigilant as we continued slowly downstream.

Soon the current picked up and the grassy swamp gave way to more defined banks and brush. We rounded a corner and came upon a ramshackle frame cabin covered in recycled tin sheeting, no doubt part of a fish camp, a good sign for salmon, anyway. I was rowing at this point, and Jack fished off the side of the raft.

"Fish on!" Jack fought it for a few minutes, obviously a nice sized fish as his rod bent double gave testimony. I headed to shore and Jack jumped off the raft and into the stream.

"It's a Dolly! Let's pull over here," he yelled. I rowed to the bank and pulled up the Metzler, tying it off to a group of alders. By the time I had my rod out of the case, Jack had landed the fish and had another one on. Quickly, I got set up and followed suit, wading into the knee to thigh deep river. Within minutes, I had a strike and both of us started whooping and hollering as our fish jumped and fought, desperately trying to spit out the hooks.

The scene repeated itself steadily—both of us landing nice sized dolly varden one after another with an occasional graying to mix things up. We probably fished for an hour before reluctantly moving on downstream and leaving the remaining fish for our bear. The rest of our float did not produce the same kind of results although we did continue to catch a few.

At one point we came around a corner in a narrower stretch of the river and found ourselves in the way of a group of local Yupik Eskimos who were fishing for salmon. Fishing is used loosely here: each of them had stout salmon rods with huge honking pixies or similarly dangerous lures probably best used for large kings. Their technique involved flipping the lures a short distance into a nearby deep hole, closing the bail with one or two winds of the handle, and then giving the rod tips some serious, quick jerks. This technique known as snagging is illegal, strictly speaking. Understand, though, that these guys don't have the luxury of going to the supermarket for easy purchases. Salmon is a main staple of their diet along with wild game from the area. They were not in it so much for the sport as dinner for the family.

Neither Jack nor I bothered to inform them about fishing regulations, however, and by the grins on their faces—part cultural and part from their results no doubt—they appeared to be having a great time. We waved and drifted on with our tiny fly rods and flies. Fishing for them is survival; for us it was fun.

136

When we got to the lower lake, Jamo stood casting in thigh deep water.

"Jesus, it took you long enough! Any luck?"

"You won't believe us—we found a GREAT hole," we both exclaimed behind huge grins, making no attempt to hide our enthusiasm. We related the experience, from the bear to the locals, providing a detailed version of the dolly fishing in the process. Since Jamo had essentially been catchless, he offered a plan.

"What are we waiting for? Let's go back." Any report of fantastic fishing brought out the gluttony in each of us.

We unpacked the raft, stowed it, and loaded up into the plane.

Arriving back at the upper lake after first ensuring with a flyover that no bears seemed to be sniffing around, Jamo determined he could taxi the plane through the channel to the stretch of river where we had discovered the dollies. Taxiing the plane slowly and carefully, we finally arrived at our hole after negotiating a few shallows and submerged boulders. We backed the plane to shore and tied it up by the cabin. We were all in a hurry to get our lines in the river and start fishing. Jamo was not disappointed.

Cries of "fish on" erupted with regularity from each of us until we tired of it and quietly continued to catch and release nice sized dollies and huge grayling. This stretch of river allowed for perfect wading as we spread out and flogged the water with non-stop action for some time.

For the next two or three hours we caught untold numbers of fish. The fish were simultaneously either rising to feed on the local hatch or exploding out of the water, hook in mouth at any given moment. At one point a passing thunderstorm dumped buckets of rain upon us but the fishing only got better. It was one of those anomalies where the setting sun shone brightly underneath the dark storm clouds overhead, and the river rippled in concentric circles from a combination of raindrops and fish breaking the surface. At day's end, we finally quit and climbed back into the plane with one or two dollies that had unfortunately mortally wounded themselves in greedy feasting on our flies. They provided a wonderful hors d' oeuvre back at the cabin in addition to our obligatory chips and guacamole. We did our traditional toast to a great day and arriving back safely, but the catching on that day was anything but ordinary.

24

Granted

The Grant River runs from Grant Lake to Kulik Lake, which forms the headwaters of the Wind and the Peace. The Grant is another short river like many that join the bodies of water in the system, probably only 6 miles or so in length as it defines a circuitous route down a short valley between the lakes. We have walked its length on several occasions, which is always a bit of a grunt. In times of high water we have successfully navigated much of its length in the Metzler. In fact, on one momentous trip with the Kellys, Jimmy and Mike screamed ahead of us in an effort to show off their navigational skills with their Zodiac. This ended in semi disaster when they swamped in a difficult section, discharging coolers, tackle boxes, and miscellaneous paraphernalia downstream. Fortunately, we were able to recover much of their gear with little damage.

Most of the time, though, we walk the river, jockeying for position as previously described. Like many of the streams in that part of Alaska, the Grant is walkable if you take precautions for a slippery bottom, boulders, deep holes, and occasionally swift current. Few spots require leaving the river and walking through the brush since the water typically gets no deeper than our waders allow. On several occasions we have walked the entire length in search of large rainbow while also scratching the itch to explore unseen parts.

Jamo's brother, Lance, along with a couple of others reportedly hiked the length of the river just to do it, and the effort was so noteworthy that they had t-shirts made reading, "We Hiked the Grant" which had the unintended result of making us feel even better about doing it in waders and fishing gear. On most occasions, Jack, Jamo, and I would hike and fish as far as a braided section, probably about halfway up the river. Here the river divided itself into various channels formed in part by beaver dams. As we continued further upriver, signs of bear activity increased and the brush became thicker, an unwelcome discovery, especially if one is unarmed—as I was. Because of that I visually tethered myself to either Jack or Jamo through those sections. At that time we had flown over the upper reaches many times but due to self-imposed limitations based on energy and time, we had not previously traveled much beyond the slower braided midsection of the river.

But as I said, the three of us eventually hiked the length of the river. The first time Jamo and I did it while Jack lagged far behind—an indicator he was catching fish. On another trip Jack and I walked to the end while Jamo stayed behind. The problem was that these hikes necessitated a tortuous return trip to the plane usually late in the evening. As tough as it was, we did not commemorate the event with even a t-shirt although we really walked it both ways.

The upper reaches of the Grant form a narrow canyon where the walking is particularly difficult on uniformly grapefruit sized boulders. Here the confined current rushes around sharp bends, and pocket eddies occasionally form around large boulders. Because we usually traveled as a group, the person or persons trailing really had little chance for catching much, but just the beauty of the river and the surrounding mountains made it worthwhile.

140

By the time Jamo and I reached the last stretches of the river near its source on that first trip to the canyon, it was getting fairly late even though the summer sun still shone brightly. The fishing had been slow in the upper reaches, and what fish we did catch tended to be small with a few exceptions. Looking upriver, we could see and hear the waterfall pouring from Grant Lake over a steep, high precipice, but the pool formed by the cascade lay hidden behind a final grassy knoll blocking our vision. Arriving at the hill, the river made a sharp right hand turn away from the knoll and circled around it, enclosed by high, sheer rocky cliffs. Jamo and I climbed the small hill and peered over the top. A basin awaited us on the other side, probably no more than 100 feet across and almost perfectly round in shape. Thousands of gallons of water noisily dumped into the basin every few seconds: we had seen it many times from the air, but the waterfall was truly impressive from ground level. Flying over it, even at low altitude did not do it justice, especially at 100 miles per hour.

Jamo ripped out several arm lengths of line and after a few false casts, sent his fly out into the middle of the basin amidst the thick fog of water airborne from the falls. Instantly a large rainbow leaped out of the water and nailed his fly, surprising us as much as it did the fish. Jamo pulled the line tight—but too late. The fish was gone after two or three tail walking leaps, only to become a late evening story back at the cabin.

Since the hour was late, we fished the pool for a few more minutes with no luck and headed back downstream, eventually running into Jack about 15 minutes behind and methodically working his way toward us. We still had a 6 mile return hike in front of us, so squinting into the late evening sun, the casting became more or less rote as we headed toward Lake Kulik and the plane. We suspected that the upper reaches of the river held promise for better fishing, but it would have to wait for another day.

25

The Art of Fly Tying

A fter my early attempts to catch fish with a variety pack of commercial flies, I became a student of bait that actually worked. I had tied flies for several years, self-taught from library books, videotape lessons, and my own misguided attempts. I purchased a used fly tying kit at a garage sale and added to its inventory through visits to fly shops and from mail order catalog purchases. Thread and sundry other household items could be bought cheaply, but I soon learned that quality fly materials were costly. Feathers, especially the "specialty" items of particular color from pheasants, peacocks, and other exotic birds, ran high. A cape of average quality hackle feathers easily ran around $20 or more at that time, but compared to the cost of individual flies, that was cheap.

I would be remiss if I compared the quality of my flies, especially in the beginning, to commercial varieties, but they caught fish and if we were in short supply of particular flies while at the cabin, it became my job to duplicate the winners. This occurred with varying degrees of success, depending on the techniques employed to create the pattern. My tools were a combination of home made dubbing needles (made from a large sewing needle, glue, and a ball point pen) and commercial implements of unclear and sometimes unknown use that came with my garage sale kit. It took research to understand, for instance, how to use a tool that looked like it belonged to a gynecologist for frogs—a "whip finisher." It cleverly wrapped the thread around the eye of the hook so that it could be cut without unraveling. This could also be accomplished with fingers, but the tool made it a snap, once I leaned how to use it. Fly tying books and inserts in magazines often give clear instructions how to tie the flies, but many times I was left to my imagination. Sometimes the results were admittedly ugly variations but they worked more often than not.

A common fly successful for fish early on, especially on the Agulapak was the Babine Special. A simple egg pattern, it consisted of a double egg shape made with orange or pink chenille and a hackle of some sort. Because it was easy to tie, it was a favorite of mine. In those early days Jack and I used lots of Babines and Wooly Buggers (or Wooly Worms as they are sometimes called), another easy-to-tie fly. Eventually though, the tying became more demanding.

My buddy, Bob Olsen, is a master fly tier—at least in my book. He would spend his winter hours at his bench tying all sorts of flies that he later gave me for Christmases, birthdays, or other celebrations. Next to mine, his flies were things of beauty. Nevertheless, my crude Frankenstein creations seemed to work, and so I filled a utilitarian function at the cabin—creating flies that caught fish—the priority regardless how homely the fly might be.

Jamo liked to experiment, and over the years the changes in flies of choice were usually the result of his experimentation. He also fished for rainbows in other venues, and this broadened his horizons as far as enticing fish to flies.

"Larry...can you add a cone head to this. This fucker won't sink, and fish seem to go crazy for my cone heads. This would be a great combination." He would be holding a furry hook, squinting for magnification, and offer it to me for inspection. His ideas usually resulted in bizarre concoctions unseen in fly shops.

Usually he wanted me to remodel an existing pattern to meet his new specifications, and I would reluctantly try to meet his specifications with the hope that no one would know who created it. The results were typically as expected: something ugly but worth a try.

Jack over the years added to his repertoire of flies as well, but basically if a fly worked for any one of us, we were all following suit—never mind the fact that experimentation might lead to even better results. If any one of us caught fish with a certain fly, you could count on the others switching immediately. Jack's calling card was a grayling fly from his youthful days—the fairy shrimp, purchased at Frontier Sporting Goods, a local sporting goods store long since out of business. Dick McIntyre, a local celebrity of sorts in the hunting and fishing world, had owned it and we grew up with his son Eddy. Mounts of wild animals from Africa and other exotic locations lined the walls of his store and gave testimony to Dick's status as a world-class hunter, no small feat in a town like Fairbanks. Like many hunting and fishing stores in small towns, it was a local hangout for old timers and wannabees. When the store closed for good, Jack purchased every last fairy shrimp in the inventory—and possibly in the world. He hoarded them like gold coins until it became apparent he would one day run out.

"Can you tie these?" Fairy shrimp were tricky. They were small and the room on the shank was tight, especially for not so nimble fat fingers. All my attempts seemed poor, at best. I could find no instructions and few references to them, and left to my own devices, my flies resembled the originals but did not actually replicate them. But then few flies actually mirror the critters they hope to fool fish with; in this case something called Anostraca (aka fairy shrimp). And even though the insect probably didn't even reside in Alaska, Jack stood by them as the mainstay of his tackle box.

Fly tiers are typically armchair entomologists by nature, but I couldn't tell a pupa from a mayfly. My choice of flies was rarely based in science, but more on gut feelings and what seemed to be working for others. Over the years I learned to keep my mouth closed regarding discussions of insects, lest my ignorance betray me.

But I did take my vise (and my vices) to the cabin each year and set up shop on the ungainly 80 pound home made fly tying table constructed with stout cedar timbers leftover from cabin construction. And as our fly choices progressed through the years, so did I. The last years we had succumbed to glitz and glamour, and the fly du jour was what Jamo named the "Christmas tree."

The Christmas tree was basically a zuddler—a streamer pattern with a cone head, spun deer hair like a muddler, a black zonker strip, a silver tinsel body, and a red throat. I could actually tie these to resemble the commercial flies. In the store, they were spendy, but never mind, you could never find any because Jamo would buy every last one in town. This fly seemed to be everything we wanted in a rainbow fly. The cone head made it sink and the tinsel and red made it sparkle, not to mention remind Jamo of the holiday season. Rainbows seemed to go crazy for the fly. Occasionally, one of us would revert to an egg-sucking leech or something else, but the cone head zuddler remained the fly of choice for many years.

An assortment of hand tied wet flies

26

Cards in the Spokes

As we aged and began to slowly understand the fishing process, our gear also morphed. I went from my fiberglass Fenwick 5-weight with a 9-weight reel—or, more accurately a 9-weight "winch," to a home made 6-weight graphite rod I had built. I had this thing about buying equipment when I could build it myself. This is both a blessing and a deficit. "I'll build it myself," is my constant refrain and even though I sometimes step in it, I am a fair craftsman. Most likely none of my woodworking projects would pass muster at the Wendell Castle school of Woodworking, but overall, my reputation is good. And while everything has a learning curve, if it is truly bad, I'll throw it out. My home built fly rod I modestly felt to be a thing of beauty.

My first home made pole was a cheap spinning rod I created in a rod building class, but confidence bolstered, I went on to buy a Lamiglas blank and built the 6-weight fly rod which I used for many years. Colorful threadwork adorned the guides, and quality materials gave it a decent look and feel. Years later, though, I received a Sage 5-weight in lieu of a gold watch for my many years teaching, and once I tried it, my home built rod was retired along with my public school teaching career. The Sage is clean and simple, but bottom line, it is a dream to use. Once smitten, I now required a backup, so I

148

bought a Sage 3-weight as well. With new reels to accompany them, I was now equipped with first class equipment.

Jack used an old fiberglass Fenwick similar to mine for many years. The tip had broken off making it a 7'4" rod instead of an 8-footer, but at least he glued a new tip-top on the end. Jamo gave him no end of shit about it, though, and finally out of embarrassment he showed up with a brand new Loomis rod and reel. With his Gore-Tex waders and Stearns fishing vest, Jack had come a long ways from a wet suit and a broken-down Fenwick rod.

Jamo from the get go carried an Orvis 9-foot 5-weight rod, which, despite the quality name, was a ball buster to cast. It could sling line a long way, and he knew how to get maximum advantage from it, but after an hour in what was usually an 8 hour day (or evening) of fishing, severe forearm agony would set in due to its horrible balance: the tip felt like it had a wrecking ball on the end. Over the years, he went through an assortment of rods to assuage the pain caused by the Orvis: some cheap Sam's Club specials and others of decent quality. The common denominator, however, to all his set ups lay not in the rod, but the reel. Price, size, quality...all were second to the "real" criteria—his reels had to make lots of noise.

When Jamo bought a reel, noise was the ONLY criteria. Oh sure, a brake was nice, and more than one spool for changing line was important, but noise was the key. As kids, we used to clothespin a playing card on our bikes to rub against the spokes—sounding like a motorcycle of sorts, or so we thought. That's how Jamo's reels all sounded. An amplifier would have been even better, but he was happy with anything that could be clearly heard by other fishermen—namely Jack and me. His original Orvis reel was loud, but he wound so much backing on it that it would jam all the time, resulting in dead quiet...and lost fish. And Jamo needed lots of backing. As long as fish were pulling line, the reel was making noise...and the longer the line, the longer the noise lasted. He made no bones about it—noisy was better. He would try other reels that were engineering marvels, but unless they made lots of noise, they were returned to the store shelves.

27

Size Matters

B esides holding a quiet reel (indicative of no fish on the line), actually losing a fish stood as the ultimate indignity. Anytime one of us had what could be clearly seen to be a "nice" fish, the automatic response from Jamo came next, "Don't horse him...you'll lose him." I think he learned this from his brother who bullied him with it, and he likewise used it to utmost leverage with Jack and me...sort of like paying it forward where the toddler picked on by an older sibling ends up taking his frustrations out on the dog.

"Jesus, you horsed him, didn't you? I knew you were going to lose him." Like water moving downhill, you could count on hearing this if a fish got off. Even worse, "Christ, that was a nice one, too. You have GOT to learn not to horse them in."

Once a fish was landed, no one in his right mind committed to stating the size of the fish. All that did was establish it as slightly smaller than everyone else's.

"God, how big was that fish?"

"At least 22 inches!"

"That's what I thought. Quite a bit smaller than mine."

And so it went.

Over the years we all caught some great fish, of course. Memories fade, but big fish stand out. I doubt if any of us ever caught anything near the record lunkers historically caught in the early spring on the Naknek River and other areas where, in one camp, nothing smaller than 30 inches is photographed, but we landed lots of beautiful rainbows on many trips. Over time we learned to photograph them with arms extended for ultimate perspective, and eventually Jack affected a standard pose with his rod clenched firmly in his teeth, giving him a somewhat primordial appearance if nothing else.

Anytime we were in sight of one another, a hooked fish garnered the attentions of the others, and the standard question would be, "What is it?"

"Rainbow" was the inevitable and immediate response until true identification could take place. Grayling and dollies were fine, but the goal was always to land a big 'bow, so unless a fish was clearly identified otherwise, every fish hooked was a rainbow until further notice.

Fishing one of our favorite holes on the Nuyakuk River, Jack hooked a nice king salmon on his 5-weight fly rod, probably a 40 pounder. Once hooked, there was no mistaking it for a rainbow, but until we could actually see it to identify it, that was exactly Jack's claim. Line screaming downstream, he was soon into his backing to where he had to chase it downstream a ways before regaining ground and bringing it back to his grassy perch. The battle took the better part of an hour, but he finally successfully landed it and we caught it on camera, Jack struggling to hold the monster with both arms, his rod gripped firmly in his teeth and only then admitting it was not a rainbow.

I'm guessing that Jamo caught the biggest rainbow that anyone actually witnessed over the years. It is hard to say since we all caught big ones from time to time, and even harder to admit, but the Kellys were there as witnesses when he pulled it out of the King Salmon River after a lengthy tail walking tussle. Never mind the dimensions—someone would just say it was slightly smaller than theirs, but out of the water it proved to be a prize. Of course any fish caught out of the sight of other fishermen did not count since, without verification, the story was assumed to be a lie.

Jamo did lose fish on occasion, but not, it seemed, as frequently as Jack or I did, especially early on. He attributed his ability to land fish to superior technique—until we figured out the "4 oz. tippet" he claimed to be using was in reality something akin to anchor line. He could pull down large trees when his fly would get caught in the brush on a back cast. Finally, I confronted him about it.

"Jamo, no fish has a chance against that rope you call fly line. We could tie the plane down with your leader."

"That light weight stuff won't turn my fly over...this is the lightest I can use," the answer was always the same.

"Your leader barely fits through the guides? What is that? Halibut line?"

Lesson learned—in time I, too, changed my ways. Following suit, I cut short my commercial leaders and replaced my spider-web thin tippet with "manly" leader. Suddenly my "landing" rate skyrocketed. All this came under the heading of my education—no longer would I use leader that breaks with the mere thought of escape—especially when your buddies are watching.

Eventually we all carried cameras for photographic evidence in case no one was around to witness a trophy as well as for future bragging rights, but taking a picture of one's own fish is difficult at best and requires dexterity and patience. The "selfies" usually do not do justice to the fish, so the preferred method is to get a partner to do the shooting while the trophy is held out as far as one's arms can reach. I was slow to learn this process, and so my early modest presentations seem diminutive compared to the depth of field perspectives offered by Jamo and Jack. At times their fish appeared bigger than the fisherman holding it—thanks to the magic of modern photography. Of course the classic pose has the fly hanging from the fish's mouth with a fly rod along side for true size comparison, but arm stretch distortions seemed to be our preferred pose. Photographic evidence notwithstanding, the end of the day discussions documenting the size of the fish only proved that memories are fleeting and fish tend to grow in proportion with the passage of time since they were caught.

Jamo with the proper fish pose

28

Necessity is a Mother

Jamo excelled throughout his life as a skier, canoeist, and various other athletic endeavors, and late in life, probably around the time of his retirement, he took up "ping pong." Of course no self respecting member of that fraternity called it that—internationally it is known as table tennis—and both Jamo and his wife Jane pursued it with profound vigor like nearly everything they do. On at least one occasion Jack and I competed with him at his house after a dinner party. First off, his equipment included not only state of the art paddles able to make the balls spin crazily out of bounds when I attempted returns, but also devices for practice and improvement—an apparatus that shot ping pong balls at the recipient with alarming speed, a table that flipped up on one end akin to practicing against a wall, and other sundry implements for improving one's game. Both Jamo and Jane regularly played in tournaments and even travelled to China as part of their enthusiasm for the sport. It was not surprising that either of them could handily defeat the likes of me, someone who has decent skills at the sport but not of the same level as these veterans.

So on one of our last trips to the cabin, we found ourselves weathered in for several days. Mike and Jimmy Kelly were also there, and while the older establishment could easily wait out the rain and fog by reading throughout the day, Jimmy became commensurately restless. He and Jamo got busy. I found myself looking up from my book at one point, to see both of them making repeated trips to the garage carrying plywood and sawhorses. Something was up.

"Jamo, what now?" I inquired.

"We're going to have a table tennis tournament," came the swift reply.

Of course this begged the obvious—what about equipment? With some piecing together various sized scraps of plywood and screwing the pieces together to 2x4 lumber, we soon had a semi-regulation table, not perfectly flat, but close enough. Now for the more difficult items to fill: Jamo had a single ping pong ball in the bottom of his clothing bag, a leftover from another trip. It was the only thing we could not have created from materials on hand, including electrical tape. For paddles, he had a ready answer.

"How about these?" He wielded a couple of iron skillets, heavy but with the requisite flat surface, at least on one side.

For a net we lined up 12 pack boxes of Pepsi across the middle of the table, and we were good to go. After a few practice sessions we adjusted things, and as long as we avoided the uneven cracks in the plywood table that produced unpredictable bounces, we were ready. Jimmy and Jamo commenced the action.

Having a bona fide professional who happens to be a retired attorney elicited reminders of the "real" rules, so Jimmy's illegal serves were quickly retired along with a few other misconceptions we harbored about scoring. We all tried our hand at it and declared the table and equipment to be a success. Naturally, individual prowess had to be proven by a tournament of champions. Jamo mapped out a bracket, and we drew for position, knowing full well that the tournament director would handily kick our respective asses...at least that was the theory.

Our bracket was double elimination and unfortunately, I drew Jamo early on. I resigned myself to early defeat, but figured I needed to save face by at least giving him a game. I had not counted on one critical factor, however: the paddles weighed a ton. Hefting frying pans considerably slowed Jamo's reflexes and leveled the playing field. In short, I beat him.

The whooping and hollering gave testimony to our unbridled enthusiasm, but it took on another dimension with Jamo's defeat by a left-handed amateur. He took it like a man, though, no doubt burning inside, and we proceeded to work through the brackets. Since we started with a round robin bracket, we were able to size up each other's strengths and weakness as spectators. Mike, our elder statesman, appeared to be the weakest, at least initially, so when my turn came up to play him, I was a bit overconfident. Suddenly, his competitive nature came out, and Mike turned into a tenacious table tennis titan—all the more so since he was playing a left handed liberal. In the end, I eventually narrowly defeated him, but we all gained sudden and newfound respect for reflexes we had never seen before. Competition brought out hidden qualities from each of us.

In the end, I won the battle of the frying pans, but it was a hollow victory. Jamo withdrew at the end, claiming wrist problems from hefting skillets, and since that is where his arthritis typically flares up, we allowed his departure begrudgingly. He awarded me the trophy, but it was a penultimate victory—Jack still had final say.

During our break from the excitement and a return to reading, Jimmy got busy. In no time he had created two crude, but definitely usable plywood paddles, complete with electrical tape around the handles for a true comfort fit. Another tournament bracket appeared. I could not rest on my laurels.

With wooden paddles, the dynamics changed. The games became faster and increasingly competitive. Suddenly, each of us took on looks of serious concentration as sweat flowed freely. Nothing was taken for granted. In the end, Jack, who had, it turned out, been clandestinely playing regularly at the university in his free time, mastered all of us and walked away with the final trophy.

Thankfully, the weather broke not long after that, and we could resume our normal routines of fishing and story telling.

29

High Anxiety

N o Alaskan fishing story would be complete without a bear story, and while bears were relatively rare occurrences, over the years we did see a number of them. Usually, we spotted them a fair distance away, but nevertheless they elicited excitement and readiness. The sighting of bears caused guns to be grabbed and a wide berth plotted. Most of the time we would see them on a riverbank from the inflatable, and the immediate evasive action was to pull up to the opposite shore and watch the bruin until we deemed it safe to proceed. Most of the rivers are shallow enough that a bear could easily charge us in the river if so desired. Invariably, though, they would eventually see or smell us, peer in our direction for confirmation, and then jog off, occasionally stopping and rechecking to see if we were still there. Sometimes we saw black bears but most of the sightings were grizzlies.

The exception to the typical bear sighting occurred on the Grant River. We had a number of favorite holes on the Grant, and being the first to arrive at any of them was a decided advantage. Leapfrogging up the stream, a certain amount of strategy decided who arrived first. Each of us knew the river well—and even though conditions changed from time to time, certain places proved themselves worthy year in and year out.

A steady rain fell as we progressed up the river. Each of us had a rain jacket hood pulled up to ward off the precipitation. This also resulted in muffling the normal river sounds. I had successfully put myself in the lead position approaching one of the key fishing holes—a bend in the river with a fair sized gravel bar and deadfall on the opposite shore. The rainbows liked to hide under the trees and brush lying in the river, sinisterly waiting for anything swept around the corner and into their lair. Fishing was tricky because the river narrowed here, and a fisherman was easily spotted. Thick brush defined the river on either bank, so walking took place in the river except where the gravel bar started.

In order to get to the gravel bar, we had to wade through a deep hole in the river that challenged the tops of our waders. I carefully descended into the hole, tiptoeing through the water, holding my pole in one hand and pulling up my sagging waders with the other to keep the water out. Climbing out of the creek and onto the bar, I slowly worked my way upstream, letting my fly drift under trees and brush and careful to keep it from snagging. A snagged fly would result in either losing the tackle or scaring off the fish. I turned and saw that Jamo was shortly behind me. He had more or less unofficially claimed this hole as his own in earlier expeditions, and no doubt he did not want me fishing out the area before he had a chance at it, so he was doing his best to nonchalantly catch me without actually appearing to be in a hurry.

I continued toward the bend watching my fly drift lazily in the current, pulling it out and quietly flipping it back upstream just before it got in the thick of the snags. By the time I reached the corner, Jamo was climbing out of the water onto the gravel bar, no doubt anxious to get to the hole I had been fishing. I continued upstream and as I rounded the corner, I looked up. Just at that moment a huge grizzly walked out of the brush upstream from me about 20 feet away.

Twenty feet seemed like five—the bear glanced back at me—but in no hurry to follow it, I yelled, "Bear" and backed quickly around the corner. In a flash, Jamo had his shotgun off his back, pumped a shell in the chamber, and fired a shot in the air. I was unarmed, and the presence of his shotgun provided a modicum of reassurance—the closer the better. I hastened to get next to him. Jamo was now on full alert, the shotgun cradled in both hands and his pole on the ground. "Where is it?" He had not seen it and was simply reacting to my warning shout.

We were now on the downstream side of the bend and due to the thick brush lining the riverbank and gravel bar, we could not see around the corner where I had spotted the bruin.

"He was just around the corner. I think he crossed the river." I permitted the shotgun to take my spot in the lead.

The river was only about 30 feet wide here so a crossing would only take seconds. Our ears ringing from the shotgun blast, we both gingerly inched forward, me in the rear, and peered around the corner like an Elmer Fudd/Bugs Bunny cartoon. Nothing. No bear. Only an empty river stood before us.

"It was a big one...check this out!" I pointed out a faint bear print in the sand that dwarfed our footprints as proof that I had not been hallucinating. We stood there for a minute or two quietly surveying the brush. Nothing...no bear, no movement...only the sounds of the river gurgling by us. By then, Jack was in view coming up the river, his .44 unholstered and pointing skyward. A shotgun blast was a rare event, and his eyes were wide open by now.

"Bear...hey bear...hey bear," he yelled out as he made his way to the bar where we stood.

I explained what had just happened, and after brief discussion, we decided lunch might be in order. My nervous system had been upgraded to high alert, but the presence of two firearms offered some solace. We pulled out our sandwiches and settled down with a snack. Jamo had already eaten most of his lunch and after munching on a few Cheez-its, got up and started fishing. A few fish gave up in customary fashion and we decided that the grizzly had probably moved on from the hole. We followed suit figuring it would avoid us. Nevertheless, we stayed within easy shouting distance of one another as we moved up the creek. Each of us shouted "Hey, bear" at regular intervals just to be on the safe side.

I was now content to let Jamo or Jack take the lead position since my fly rod was my only weapon, and I doubted that an egg sucking leech on a #8 hook was any match for a grizzly bear. From where I had first seen the bear, the river wound through a brushy area and then further upstream formed a deep hole underneath a severe cut bank. About a quarter mile above that, it broke into numerous braided smaller channels through heavy brush. From previous hikes I remembered it as serious bear country with prevalent bear signs and thick alder and willow to camouflage animals.

The deep hole ahead of us had produced nice fish in the past, and Jack was first to arrive. Immediately he had a heavy strike, but both Jamo and I immediately recognized it as a red salmon and not a feisty rainbow. Jamo slipped around and above Jack on the western edge of the river and let his fly drift down into the hole. The deep pool under the cut bank was filled with reds, but the rainbows mingle with them in hopes of an egg meal. After a quick cast into the pool Jamo had a big rainbow on.

The rain had by now reasserted itself into a steady drizzle. I slipped up ahead of Jamo by walking around and behind him.

Larry Meath

While both Jamo and Jack faced the pool on the eastern bank, I traversed the river upstream to the opposite side and cast my fly toward the western bank. My back was against the cut bank, essentially a sheer wall, but the western bank above Jamo and Jack now had a deeper channel where I hoped some fish might be hiding. The bank opposite me was covered in dense brush, and because the river had narrowed in the stretch above the pool, the current fairly sped toward the corner and gurgled noisily over the rock bottom. It wasn't a particularly great spot, but Jamo and Jack had the hole covered so my plan was to work up the cut bank to the head of the riffle.

Suddenly, my plans changed.

A roar thundered across the stream, drowning the river and rain noises instantly. Shocked by the magnitude of the sound, I looked up to see a grizzly charging out of the brush in a beeline for me, the fur on its back standing straight up and large canines bared in a menacing snarl. It jumped out of the brush, off the bank, and into the river at full speed. The river was probably 50 or 75 feet wide here, and quick mental calculations suggested that—basically—I was screwed. My back literally and figuratively to the wall, I looked downstream and in what seemed like slow motion, saw Jamo and Jack still fighting their fish, backs to me. In a nanosecond, I mustered all my wit, ingenuity, and bravery and—screamed—probably like a little girl—a blood curdling, hysterical, scream like when someone jumps out of a dark closet at you and says boo. My thoughts were crystal clear, though: "This is going to be really ugly."

A charging grizzly is capable, so I've been told, of outrunning a quarter horse for short distances. No matter the equation, I had no time to do anything except duck and pray. My only defense lay useless in my left hand, a 6-weight fly rod I had carefully constructed on my own, but had forgot to add a

163

30.06 option to the butt. In two or three strides, the brute was within 15 feet of me. That's when I heard the explosion.

Suddenly the bear stopped on a dime in the middle of the river. I'd be lying if I said I could smell his breath, but I'm certain he could smell at least a part of me. The explosion did not incapacitate the bear in any way, though. It simply gave him pause. It now turned downstream as if deciding who was the tastiest, Jamo or me. Jamo stood there, shotgun in both hands and eyes as big as the proverbial saucers—undoubtedly he was rethinking his decision to bring attention to himself.

Then, just as quickly as it started, it ended. The bear spun quickly on its back legs, hustled off into the brush, and disappeared instantly.

My feet shuffled downstream as rapidly as I could move them in order to get next to the shotgun. Jamo's rod was lying in the water with line going in every direction. Below us, Jack once again had his pistol out and pointed skyward ready to shoot down anything that moved. None of us had relaxed just because the bear had run into the brush.

"Jesus," was all I could say. We stood there for a minute making sure no encores occurred and peering into the dense vegetation. After some time we deemed it safe once again and breathed.

"Grab my rod," Jamo ordered. He was not going to let go of his shotgun. I caught his Orvis pole and started winding his line in as the current slowly carried it downstream. The rainbow was temporarily still on his fly but managed to spit the hook before I could get the line tight again.

"Holy shit," I exclaimed. "How close was that?"

"Close enough I couldn't shoot the bear without hitting you!" Jamo was only about 50 feet below me, but he was convinced the grizzly was too close to take a shot, so he fired in the air. The rule of thumb is that if a bear is charging, a bluff will break off at about 20 feet. Inside of that they usually mean business. This was clearly within that margin.

I retold what I had seen, not failing to mention that Jamo had been fishing with his back to me during the episode. "How did you know to turn around?" I asked. "Did you see him charge?"

"I heard the roar first and when I turned, I saw him charging. I dropped my rod and got the shotgun off my back in a hurry," Jamo explained. "There was no time to try and shoot him by then—he was too close to you—so I fired in the air. I almost regretted it when he stopped and looked like he was coming for me."

We continued staring into the brush, praying the event didn't repeat itself. "I'm not sure that was the same bear from below," I added. "The first bear seemed bigger." Common sense would mandate that it was the same bear, and not that it made any difference, but the first bear seemed huge—like a true coastal Brown bear. Bears close to the coast feast on a diet of salmon and take on huge proportions as a result. This bear was plenty big enough...especially in a full charge, snarling and snapping and fur on end. As beneficiary of that charge, I wasn't going to quibble on whether I had seen one or two different bears—I was just happy to be still standing. The prospect of two bears instead of one did not calm any of us.

"I'm voting we head downstream back to the plane. Personally, I've had enough excitement for one day." I had little desire at this point to continue upriver, especially into the braided section of river above us. All things considered, little argument came from either Jack or Jamo. Jack was now standing next to us. His pistol seemed like a pea-shooter after watching a grizzly in full charge, but it was better than nothing.

"Am I ever happy you were able to get that shotgun off your back in a hurry. It was looking grim...in fact, I'm not sure how you managed it." As I recounted the event in my head, it seemed impossible that Jamo could have dropped his rod, removed the shotgun, turned and fired in the split second of the incident. Fortunately, he didn't have to pump a shell into the chamber since he had done that with the first sighting.

We later replicated the situation when we finally got back to the cabin, and Jamo repeatedly demonstrated his quick draw technique. His sling attached to either end of the short barrel pistol grip 12 gauge was wrapped diagonally across his chest so that the shotgun rode upside down on his back. From this position he was able to drop his rod, slip the strap over his head while spinning it so that the gun ended up in the ready position in the blink of an eye—or more accurately, in the blink of a charging bear.

For the return trip downstream, my fly did not return to the water for some time. Jack and Jamo occasionally made lackluster casts into a passing hole or under a tree, but the spirit of fishing seemed to have disappeared.

"Just think how close you came to ruining our trip," Jamo philosophized. Jack and I would have had to carry your bloody carcass all the way back to the plane and even then the rest of the trip would probably have been ruined." Jamo's sympathy nearly brought a tear to my eye.

The rest of the walk downstream was pretty much the same—me taking massive shit from both of them as well as enduring rude comments about checking my shorts and similar scatological references. As we neared the mouth, the weather worsened. A low bank of clouds had formed solidly around the nearby peaks.

When we finally arrived at the lake, departure seemed iffy at best. The rain beat steadily in a constant drizzle, but more importantly, no horizon was visible. Typically we would take off to the east over a series of fairly low hills and then head due south to Aleknagik and the cabin. However, the eastern end of the lake was covered in clouds and fog. A western departure down the lake would take us to the headwaters of the Wind and the Peace and then on to Lake Beverly, but that canyon was relatively narrow to begin with and surrounded by tall mountains.

We loaded up and taxied out into the lake, not so much in preparation for takeoff as to scout out a suitable place to camp. Lake Kulik had little in the way of decent camping spots with its steep shoreline, but just down the lake from the river mouth we spotted a grassy bank that appeared to be relatively level. It did not look to have much in the way of firewood, but the other favorable factors swayed us and we taxied ashore.

Once the tent had been pitched and our emergency supplies unloaded, we changed clothes, fixed a bite to eat from our freeze dried rations, and got in out of the rain. Darkness began to settle in with the late hour and cloud cover, so the decision was made to spend the night—hence the whiskey appeared. We had no ice, of course, and so, drinking it neat, we toasted the day and ruminated on the events one more time.

I had still not acquired a taste for whiskey, but there was no way I was not going to have a drink. Jamo poured me a dollop of Jack Daniels in my tin cup and I took a swig. As the amber liquid burned a passage down my throat, I posed the question, "So, Jack—from your perspective, how close was that bear?"

Jack thought for a second. As an engineer, he was not given to exaggeration, veracity being his strong suit except when describing the size of his fish. But then, that is a pardonable sin.

"Larry..." he paused," I thought you were a goner." His succinct appraisal verified my own feelings. Jamo nodded affirmation as he sipped his whiskey. More jokes ensued concerning their near brush with a ruined trip, but eventually we lay quietly until the reverie was broken by Jamo's buzz saw snoring. Jack, less noisy but nonetheless off in Neverland, followed suit. I stared at the translucent fabric of the tent and relived the moment like a film loop continuously playing over and over in my head. The rain continued to fall. It was definitely good to be alive.

And I carried a shotgun after that.

30

The End of an Era

Eventually and inevitably, good things must end. For us it came at the intervention of a governmental bureaucracy and aging bodies. Jamo was a top-notch pilot in my book: an opinion reinforced by many of the previous stories and the fact that we were all still alive. He was also a stickler for regulation and doing things by the book. Late in the history of our trips together, he discovered during a visit to the doctor for a routine physical that he suffered from arterial blockage, and after a stress test to confirm the diagnosis, he had a stint placed in the artery to normalize the blood flow around his heart. As a result, we missed a year of fishing until he could get FAA clearance for his physical.

However, after a year's absence from our trip we once again resumed our migration as normal. Jamo's health appeared to be better than ever and with his retirement from law practice, he seemed in the peak of shape both mentally and physically. Doctors continued to give him a clean bill, and our trips only became better with age. That is until the long arm of the law intervened.

Prior to our last trip Jamo submitted to the FAA all the appropriate paperwork for his yearly physical to maintain his pilot's license. However, he had not received confirmation that the license had been renewed by the day of our departure for

Dillingham. "It's only a formality," he explained. "Everything has been turned in, so we're going anyway."

Neither Jack nor I gave it any thought. A pilot's license was just a piece of paper to us, and in truth, hundreds of pilots in Alaska don't even bother getting a license. Jamo, though, was clearly burdened by not having the process completed as evidenced by his mention of it during the trip.

The trip went flawlessly—no bears, decent weather, great fishing at times, and we all returned intact. It was a couple of weeks later when the bad news hit. I received a call from Jamo.

"Larry—Jamo here. I've got some bad news!"

"What's up?" I figured his wife had beaten him at table tennis...a passion for both of them.

"The FAA wants me to redo my physical."

Surely, this was an inconvenience, but I failed to see this as any kind of monumental hurdle, especially since our trip was out of the way. I waited for more.

"Fuck it, I'm not going to do it...it's too much of a hassle anymore." Jamo's voice was resolute. "We've had a good run and we're all still alive, so I'm calling it quits."

And that was that. Oh, I questioned him about the plane, the cabin sitting idle, etc., but the Rubicon had been crossed...the die cast. As a pilot, Jamo was finished.

I later called Jack who had not heard the news yet. It was received much like the decisions to wait out the weather on a gravel bar—with grave acceptance. Jamo was not the wishy-washy type. And, in fact, that is exactly what happened: he quit flying. Since both his brothers had basically given up flying long ago, and since both of them were fitted with similar stints in their arteries for their own health reasons, it was a foregone conclusion that the plane would be sold. And eventually it was.

But actually, the trips have not completely ended. Since that decision, Jack and Jamo have returned to the area, travelling by way of commercial airlines and charters. I have been unable to go due to timing and work issues, and I worry somewhat that I may never get back. Logistics get complicated with the addition of bodies. They have been dropped off in the upper reaches of our favorite rivers and floated down to a predetermined pick-up spot where they meet their chartered flight back to the cabin or to Dillingham. Friendly locals have hauled them back and forth across the lake, so really, it has worked out fairly well.

Jack informed me that he even learned something new the last trip: Jamo will stoop to drink Canadian whiskey as he had to do when he ran out of Jack Daniels on the last days of their float. I have not heard Jamo's version, but he will have a spin on it that leaves him blameless, no doubt.

Of course, the trip is not really the same—no more late night flights back to the cabin for food, drink, and bragging rights. The flying, as routine as it may have seemed, was part of the adventure not to mention a never-ending source of beautiful vistas. Many of the creature comforts are gone, but camping outdoors need not be uncomfortable. Home now is a tent on the river with whatever nature offers in the way of weather, and that's not so bad. And yet the fishing is still the same: always great—even when the catching is slow.

Nonetheless, it marks a page turned—a period of my life filled with unforgettable memories, experiences only we who shared them can understand even though they are not unlike those of generations of fishermen before us. But in the end, we each have our own versions and perceptions. I wouldn't change anything—the rubber waders, the lost fish, the pike feast—even the bear attack. It has been a great ride with two wonderful friends...two of the most trustworthy liars with whom anyone would ever want to associate.

Trustworthy Liars: Jamo and Jack

Acknowledgments

As with many things in life, this project came about through luck and serendipity. I've been a writer on a small scale all my life, but publishing a work is a completely different matter. Baring one's soul has its own hazards and benefits, and in the end the process was rewarding—at least for me.

I owe thanks to many for their help along the way. Ed Thompson gave me the original motivation to ink these stories, and I apologize to him for abusing his camera afterwards with unplanned photos that must have taken him by surprise. Bob Olsen has been a reminder to me that life is short and we need to drink the good stuff first. My wife Stephanie is ever faithful and supportive of most everything I do. There is a reason why my friends call her St. Stephanie.

Specifically, I have a huge debt of gratitude to Kent Sturgis, or Big Otis as he has been known to me since our childhood. His years of experience in the publishing business provided me with detailed criticisms about how to improve my clunky first efforts and loosen some of the language. In the same vein, Sarah Norton scrutinized portions of this, and for a mere bottle of wine she provided me with much of the same kind of help. It was a pleasure to sit down with someone whom I watched grow up and realize what a talent she has turned out to be.

Of course none of these adventures would have been possible without the camaraderie of Jamo and Jack who read the initial manuscript and did not wince too obviously. Their corrections about details fogged by age and memory aided me greatly. And, they are the source of the stories.

Finally, my thanks to the fish that refused to spit out the hook and made my day before I humbly returned them to the water.

Made in the USA
San Bernardino, CA
15 March 2016